THE SPIRITUAL GROUND OF EDUCATION

[XV]

The Foundations of Waldorf Education

RUDOLF STEINER

THE SPIRITUAL GROUND OF EDUCATION

Lectures presented in Oxford, England
August 16–29, 1922

Anthroposophic Press

Published by Anthroposophic Press
400 Main Street
Great Barrington, MA 01230
www.steinerbooks.org

Translated with permission from Rudolf Steiner's *Die geistig-seelischen Grundkräfte der Erziehungskunst* (GA 305), copyright © 1991 Rudolf Steiner–Nachlassverwaltung.

This revised edition copyright Anthroposophic Press © 2004

Publication of this work was made possible by a grant from
THE WALDORF CURRICULUM FUND.

All rights reserved. No part of this book may be reproduced in any form without the written permission of the publishers, except for brief quotations embodied in critical articles and reviews.

ISBN 0-88010-513-5

Library of Congress Cataloging-in-Publication Data

Steiner, Rudolf, 1861–1925.
 [Geistig-seelischen Grundkräfte der Erziehungskunst. English]
 The spiritual ground of education : lectures presented in Oxford, England, August 16-29, 1922 / Rudolf Steiner.
     p. cm. — (The foundations of Waldorf education ; 15)
 Includes bibliographical references and index.
 ISBN 0-88010-513-5 (alk. paper)
 1. Education — Philosophy. 2. Waldorf school of education. I. Title. II. Series.
LB775.S7S73 2003
370'.1— dc21
                                                          2003006435

Contents

Introduction by Christopher Bamford	*vi*
1. The Spiritual Ground of Education *August 16, 1922*	*1*
2. The Perception of Soul and Spirit *August 17, 1922*	*15*
3. The Spiritual Ground of Physical Education *August 18, 1922*	*28*
4. The Art of Educating Young Children *August 19, 1922*	*43*
5. The Art of Educating Older Boys and Girls *August 21, 1922*	*58*
6. Teachers As Artists in Education *August 22, 1922*	*74*
7. The Organization of the Waldorf School *August 23, 1922*	*88*
8. Moral Teaching & Eurythmy in the Waldorf School *August 24, 1922*	*105*
9. Teachers in the Waldorf School *August 25, 1922*	*121*
The Foundations of Waldorf Education	*136*
Rudolf Steiner's Lectures and Writings on Education	*138*
Bibliography and Further Reading	*141*
Index	*142*

Introduction

Christopher Bamford

THE SPIRITUAL GROUND OF EDUCATION is exceptional among Rudolf Steiner's many lectures on Waldorf education for its breadth, depth, daring, and accessibility. Given in 1922 at Mansfield College, Oxford, England, the audience was one of the most prestigious that Steiner ever addressed. The occasion was a conference on "Spiritual Values in Education and Social Life." About two hundred people attended. Dr. Millicent Mackenzie, then Professor of Education at Cardiff—a person for whom Steiner had the highest regard—was in the chair throughout the lectures. The Minister for Labor, Dr. H. A. L. Fisher presided. Other lecturers included celebrated names such as Gilbert Murray, the great classicist, A. Clutton Brock, the essayist, Professor Maxwell Garnett, and Edward Holmes.

Nevertheless, despite this luminous company, the *Oxford Chronicle* reported that "The most prominent personality at the Congress is probably Dr. Rudolf Steiner." Dr. Jacks, Principal of Manchester College, welcomed the conferees, and he, too, singled out Rudolf Steiner "whom he designated as the principal personality at the Congress." The *Chronicle* reports: "Dr. Jacks said that the writings of Dr. Steiner impressed him as something extraordinarily stimulating and valuable."

Writing on August 21, a national daily, *The Manchester Guardian*, concurred:

> The entire congress finds its central point in the personality and teaching of Dr. Rudolf Steiner, and through this fact the audience is especially impressed. Many of those sharing in the conference—and these come, indeed, out of the most varied lands in the world—are already eager adherents of the teachings of Dr. Steiner. Others, who heard him for the first time, received a strong impression from his personality, and look forward with intense eagerness to the further development of his theory of education in the twelve following lectures.

On August 31, after the conference was over, *The Guardian* reported:

> Dr. Rudolf Steiner's lectures, for which we express our very special thanks, brought to us in a very vivid way an ideal of humanity in education. He spoke to us about teachers who, freely and unitedly, unrestricted by external prescriptions and regimentation, develop their education methods exclusively out of thorough knowledge of human nature. He spoke to us about the kind of knowledge needed by the teacher, a knowledge of the being of man and the world, which is at the same time scientific and also penetrates into the most intimate inner life, which is intuitive and artistic.

In other words, Rudolf Steiner rose magnificently to the occasion. Clearly enthused by the opportunity to address so large and formidable a gathering, he was delighted to be able to bring conferees the good news of what was being done in Waldorf education. More generally, he also understood that the occasion was an opportunity to showcase for the British his anthroposophical "spiritual science," of which the practice of

Waldorf education was an important, even primary, application. This task was made easier by the natural pragmatism of the English audience, who, Steiner felt, could be spoken to directly, which he did every morning of the conference.

In this setting, therefore, Steiner begins by stating immediately and without hesitation that Waldorf education and its curriculum is based entirely upon spiritual-scientific knowledge of the human being. Education is, as he says, "the primary area of life in which we must come to terms with the spirit." We must understand the developing child as a whole human being—body, soul, and spirit. We learn that, in children, spirit is closer to the body than in adults. Physical nature is shaped by the spirit. All this must be taken into account. *Spiritual understanding must guide the educational process.* But this is not "esoteric" knowledge. As Steiner says, "Devoted, unprejudiced observation of life goes a long way to bringing about such understanding." Steiner gives many instances of what this can provide. At the same time, he stresses repeatedly the importance of teachers who can teach with love as well as through art. Above all, he says, Waldorf education is a preparation for life. "This must be the ground for what we might call a spiritual-physiological pedagogy. We must have a feeling for brining living things to children—things that can continue with them into later life. What we foster in children often lives imperceptibly in the depths of the soul, and in later life it emerges."

In the second lecture, the audience having had difficulty with his use of the word "spiritual" (as in "spiritual cognition"), Steiner decided to deviate from his original plan and speak directly and openly about these things. What he has to say will be of great interest and usefulness to anyone who has had the same difficulty as the original audience. Spirit, he admits, is not directly perceptible anywhere. We see only its expression—above all and most clearly in children's development, where "spiritual forces and soul essences are active in the formation of the brain and in shaping the whole organism." He adds, "What we see are manifestations of life in a child; we perceive these with our senses. But it is spirit and soul that work through them from behind the veil of sense-perceptible things." In other words: "Spirit is the reality of hidden depths.... Spirit is activity; it is always doing, it is always creative." He then gives numerous examples of this activity and how to become aware of it.

The third lecture unfolds the nature of the human being as a threefold organism. This, Steiner says, is a necessary precondition for understanding the Waldorf approach. Subsequent lectures deal with teaching younger and older children, which leads on to the whole question of education as an "art," and teachers as "artists" in education. Following from this, Steiner reports on the actual organization of Waldorf schools and moral teaching and eurhythmy. Finally, he turns again to the teacher, the core of any pedagogy. *Teachers must be exemplars of a way of life.* They must be artistic and able to improvise, free of preconceptions and forever expecting the unexpected. They must be sensitive and receptive to the changes in human nature. And, above all:

> We need open minds, ready to receive new wisdom each day, and a disposition that can transform accumulated knowledge into a sense of potential that leaves the mind clear for the new. This keeps people healthy, fresh, and active. A heart that is open to changes in life—its unexpected and continuous freshness—must be a Waldorf teachers basic nature and mood.

At the same time, the students must feel connected to their teachers. If not, something must be done. Steiner provides anecdotes and examples that show the importance of this.

All in all, *The Spiritual Ground of Education* is one of Steiner's most exciting and revealing courses on education.

The Spiritual Ground of Education

August 16, 1922

First, I ask you to forgive me for being unable to speak to you in the language of this country, and because I am unpracticed, I must form things in the language I am able to use. Any problems this causes will, I trust, be rectified in the translation that follows. Second, allow me to say that I feel especially grateful to the distinguished committee that made it possible for me to hold these lectures here at Oxford. It is a special honor to be able to lecture in this venerable town, where I experienced the grandeur of ancient tradition twenty years ago.

Now I am about to speak of a method of education that may, in a sense, be called new. These days, I would say that there are many who seek novelty simply for the sake of novelty. However, before anyone strives for something new in any area of human culture, one must first learn to respect what is old. Here in Oxford, I feel the power that lives in these old traditions and how it inspires. One who can feel this may also have the right to speak of what is new. In order to maintain itself, anything new must be rooted in the venerable past. It may be the failure and tragedy of our time that there is a constant demand for various new things, while so few are inclined to create the new from the old.

Consequently, I am deeply grateful in particular to Mrs. Mackenzie, the organizer of this conference, and to the whole committee that arranged these lectures. I feel deep gratitude because this makes it possible to express something new in this environment of revered antiquity, which alone can sponsor it. I am equally grateful for the very kind words of introduction that Principal Jacks spoke here yesterday.

I have already indicated, perhaps, the point of view from which these lectures will be given. What I have to say about education and teaching is based on the spiritual scientific knowledge that has been my life's work. Initially, this spiritual science was cultivated for its own sake, and in recent years friends have come forward to carry it into particular domains of practical life as well. Thus, it was Emil Molt of Stuttgart who, being aware of the work in spiritual science at the Goetheanum, wanted to see it applied to the education of children in a school.[1] This led to the Waldorf school in Stuttgart. The educational principles of this school are based on a spiritual life that leads necessarily to a renewed education and conforms with the spirit of our age, a renewal demanded by the tasks of human development during the present epoch.

This education and curriculum is based entirely on knowledge of the human being. This knowledge spans our whole being, from birth to death. It aims to know all the suprasensory aspects of the human being between birth and death—everything that demonstrates the human place in a suprasensory world. In our age, we have many kinds of spiritual life, but above all we have a spiritual life inherited from ancient times and handed down by tradition. Along with this spiritual life and having less and less contact with it, there is the life that flows to us from the magnificent discoveries of modern natural science. In an age that includes the lives of the leading spirits of

---

1. Emil Molt (1876–1936), industrialist who initiated the first Waldorf school for his workers' children in Stuttgart.

natural science, when speaking of spiritual life we cannot ignore the potent contributions of natural science to knowledge of the human being.

Natural science can indeed help us understand the bodily nature and functions of the human being during physical life. It has not, however, succeeded in reaching the essential spirit of the human being, because it experiments with external tools and observes with the outer senses. I do mean this as a criticism. It was the great service of natural science (as systematized by people like Huxley, for example) that it looked at nature, with complete disregard of anything spiritual in the world.[2] Nevertheless, the knowledge of the human being derived from psychology and anthropology cannot help us understand anything spiritual. In our modern civilization, we have a spiritual life, and the various religious denominations maintain and spread this life of the spirit. However, that spiritual culture is incapable of answering the essential questions about eternity and immortality or about the suprasensory life to which we belong. It does not give us confidence when our isolation in worldly life causes us to wonder about the true nature of the eternal, suprasensory reality behind the world of the senses.

We may have beliefs about our existence in the womb of divine suprasensory worlds before we were born. We may form beliefs about what our souls will go through after passing through the portal of death. And we may formulate such beliefs into a creed that warms our hearts and cheers our spirits. We can tell ourselves that, within the universe as a whole, we are greater beings than we are in this physical life between birth and death. But what we gain is still a belief, something we

---

2. Thomas H. Huxley (1825–1895), *The Elements of Physiology and Hygiene; A Text-Book for Educational Institutions* (1868).

think and feel. It is becoming increasingly difficult to put into practice the great discoveries and principles of natural science while holding on to such spiritual beliefs. Whereas we know of the spirit, we no longer understand how to utilize spirit or do anything with it, nor do we know how to permeate our work and daily life with spirit.

And what is the primary area of life in which we must come to terms with spirit? It is education. Here we must comprehend the whole human being, which is body, soul, and spirit. We must be able to work with spirit when we teach. In every era, people have had to take spirit into consideration and work through its power. Now, because we have made such advances in the physical sciences, this call to work with spirit is even more urgent. Consequently, today's social issue is primarily one of education. Today we may ask ourselves, justifiably, what we can do that will make our society and social institutions less tragic and menacing. We have only one answer: those who have been educated through the creative activity of spirit must be given positions in the practical life of the community.

The sort of knowledge we are speaking of assumes that we continue to deal with life. It looks for the spirit within life and makes this the basis of education through the stages of life. In children, spirit is closer to the body than in adults, and we see in children how physical nature is shaped by spirit. What exactly is a child's brain at the time of birth according to modern natural science? It is like a sculptor's clay, ready for shaping. Now look at the brain of a seven-year-old at the beginning of elementary school; it has become a wonderful work of art, but one that will need more work, right up to the end of schooling. Hidden spiritual forces work to mold the human body, and as educators we are called on to contribute to this work. We are called to do more than observe bodily nature; whereas we must never neglect the body, we are asked to observe the way spirit is at work in bodily nature. We are called to work with the unconscious spirit, to link ourselves not only with the natural, but with the divine order of the world.

When we confront education earnestly, we must do more than acknowledge God for the peace of our souls; we must also will God's will and act on the intentions of God. This, however, requires a spiritual basis in education. It is this that I will speak to you about in the following days.

When we observe children, we must feel how necessary it is to have spiritual understanding and vision before we can adequately follow what takes place in them each day—what takes place in the soul and spirit. We should consider how the very youngest children are completely different in later childhood, let alone adulthood. We should bear in mind the great amount of sleep children need in their early days of life. We must wonder what takes place in that interchange between spirit and body when a baby spends nearly twenty-two hours asleep. Today, in both philosophy and practical life, it is thought that one can no more see into the soul of a child than one can see into the soul of an animal or plant—here we encounter the limit of human knowledge.

The spiritual view that we represent here does not say that these are the limits of human knowledge, or human cognition. Rather, we must bring forth from the depths of human nature the forces of cognition that can observe the complete human being of body, soul, and spirit—just as a physiologist can observe the structure of the human eye or ear. If, until now, we lack such knowledge because of our natural scientific education, we must begin to build it up. Consequently, I will speak to you about how to develop a kind of knowledge that assures genuine insight into the inner texture of childhood life. Devoted, unprejudiced observation of life goes a long way in bringing about such understanding.

If we look at a child and see only the outer, we cannot find any specific points of development between birth and about the twentieth year. We see everything only as a continuous development. But this is not true of one who observes childhood through the knowledge I will speak of during the next few days. In this case, children up to the seventh or eighth year, when the change of teeth begins, are fundamentally different from what they are later on, after the change of teeth until about the fourteenth year, or puberty. We are confronted by very significant questions when we try to sink deep into a child's life. How do soul and spirit work on children up to the change of teeth? How do soul and spirit work on children when we have to educate them at the elementary school level? How should we cooperate with soul and spirit?

We see, for example, that speech develops instinctively during the first period of life, up to the change of teeth—instinctively, as far as children are concerned and regarding their surroundings. We devote a good deal of thought today to the question of how children learn to speak. (I will not go into the historical origin of speech today.) But how do children actually learn to speak? Do they have some sort of instinct whereby they lay claim to the sounds they hear? Or do they derive the impulse for speech from some other connection with their environment? If we look more deeply into childhood life, we can see that children learn to speak by imitating what they observe unconsciously in their surroundings, using the senses. The whole life of children, up to the seventh year, is a continuous imitation of events in their environment. And the moment they perceive something, whether a movement or a sound, an impulse arises as an inner gesture to relive, with the intensity of their whole inner nature, what has been perceived.

We can understand children only when we contemplate them as we would the eye or ear of an older person, because the whole being of a child is a sense organ. Blood pulses through a child's body in a far livelier way than it does later on in life. By means of a fine physiology, we can perceive the basis for the development of our sense organs—the eye, for example. During the very early years, blood assumes primacy in the process of the eye's development. Later, the nerves begin to predominate more and more. The structure of the human senses develops from blood circulation to nerve activity. It is possible to acquire a delicate faculty for perceiving how the blood system gradually leads into the nervous system.

As with a single sense organ (say, the eye), so goes the whole human being. Children need a great deal of sleep because they are like a whole sense organ; they would otherwise be unable to endure the dazzle and noise of the outer world. Just as the eye must close to the dazzling sunlight, likewise this sense organ—the child—must shut itself off against the world. Because children are like an entire sense organ, they must sleep a great deal. Whenever children are confronted with the world, they have to observe and converse inwardly. Every sound of speech arises from an inner gesture.[3]

Let me say that what I am saying here out of spiritual knowledge is open to scientific demonstration today. There is a scientific discovery—and please forgive the personal allusion, but this discovery has dogged me all my life; it is just as old as I am, having been made the year I was born. This discovery has to do with the fact that human speech depends on the left parietal convolution of the brain. It is formed in the brain. This whole development takes place, however, during childhood by means of the formative forces I have spoken of. And if we contemplate the whole connection between the gestures of the right arm

---

3. For a more extensive discussion of his ideas on language, see Rudolf Steiner, *The Genius of Language: Observations for Teachers* (Anthroposophic Press, 1995).

and the right hand (which usually dominate in children), we can see how speech is formed out of gesture through imitation of the environment, using an inner, secret connection between blood, nerves, and brain convolutions. Later, I will speak of left-handed children and their relation to the majority; they are exceptional, but they prove very well how the building forces of speech are connected with every gesture of the right arm and hand, right down to smallest details.

If we had a more subtle physiology than is usual today, we would be able to discover not only the passive but the active principle for each phase of life. The active principle is especially alive in the child as a great organ of sense. Thus children live in their environment in the same way that, in later years, one's eye lives in its environment. The eye is formed from the general organization of the head. It lies in a separate cavity so that it can participate in the life of the outer world. Likewise, children participate in the life of the outer world; they live entirely within the external world and do not yet sense themselves.

Today, the kind of knowledge we develop is called intellectual knowledge, and it is entirely within us. It is the form of knowledge appropriate to our civilization. We believe we comprehend the outer world, but the thoughts and logic to which we limit knowledge dwell within us. Children, on the other hand, live entirely outside themselves. Do we have the right to claim that our intellectual mode of knowledge ever allows us to participate in a child's experience of the outer world—this child who is all sense organ? We cannot do this. We can only hope to achieve this through a kind of cognition that goes beyond itself—one that can enter the nature of all that lives and moves. *Intuitional* cognition is the only knowledge that can do this. Not intellectual knowledge, which leaves us within ourselves; that knowledge causes us to question every idea in terms of its logic. We need a knowledge that allows spirit to penetrate the depths of life itself—*intuitional* knowledge. We must consciously acquire *intuitional* knowledge; only then can we become practical enough to do what we must in relation to spirit in children during their earliest years.[4]

Now, as children gradually change teeth, and in place of the inherited teeth they begin to show those that were formed during the first period of life, a change comes about in their life as a whole. Now they are no longer entirely sense organ, but they are given up more to a soul element than to their sensory impressions. Children of elementary school age no longer absorb what they observe in their environment; now they take in what lives in the objects of observation. They enter a stage that should be based primarily on the principle of authority— the authority children encounter in teachers.

Let's not deceive ourselves by thinking that the children between seven and fourteen whom we are educating do not adopt the judgments we express. If we make them listen to a judgment we express in a certain phrase, we present them with something that properly belongs only to a later age. The true nature of children wants to be able to believe in us. They want to have an instinctive feeling that this is someone who can tell me something. They want to believe that teachers can inform them, because they are so connected with the whole world that they can tell. Children want to see teachers as mediators between themselves and the whole universe. This is how children confront teachers, though not of course in so many words, but instinctively. For children, adults are the mediators between the divine world and themselves in their dependence.

---

4. Steiner uses the words *imagination, inspiration,* and *intuition* in very specific ways to describe levels of initiation, or spiritual capacities. Therefore, to distinguish his use of these words from their more common meanings, they are italicized in this volume. For clear descriptions of Steiner's use of these terms, see *Stages of Higher Knowledge* (Anthroposophic Press, 1967).

The only true educators are those who are aware that they must, as a matter of course, be this kind of authority; children must be able to look up to them in a perfectly natural way.

So we have found in the course of our Waldorf school teaching and education that the question of education is principally one of teachers. How can teachers become natural authorities, mediators between the divine order of the world and children? What has the child become? From around seven to fourteen or or fifteen, children go from being all sense organ to becoming all soul. They are not yet spirit, when they place the highest value on logical connections, or intellect, because this would cause an inner ossification of the soul. For children between seven and fourteen, it is far more significant to tell them about something in a kind and loving way than it is to demonstrate by proof. During lessons, kind humor and congeniality are far more valuable than logic. Such children do not yet need logic; they need us and our humanity.

We can say that, just as children are imitators in their early years, in later years they become followers, whose souls develop according to what they can experience in soul within their psychic environment. Their sense organs have now become independent. The soul of these children has only now come into its own, and we must treat this soul with infinite tenderness. As teachers, we must become continually more intimate with what happens day by day in children's souls. Hence, in the Waldorf school, we place the greatest importance on the ability of those who teach children from seven to fourteen to give them what is appropriate for their age, with artistic love and loving art. It is essential to the education we are speaking of that teachers know the human being, and that they know what each age requires of us in teaching. What is required for the first year? What is required up to the seventh year? What is required during the elementary school period? The way we educate children up to the tenth year must be quite different; and again we must use different methods when we introduce them to human knowledge between ten and fourteen. The spiritual ground of education requires that we hold in our souls a lively image of a child's nature for each year, and even each week.

In this introductory talk today, I will indicate only one thing. For every child, there is a critical point during the school years. There is a critical moment, roughly between the ninth and eleventh years, that must not be overlooked by teachers. During this age, every normal child reaches a moment when a certain question arises: How do I find my place in the world? One must not imagine that this question arises just as I have said it. It arises as vague, unsatisfied feelings. The question reveals itself through a child's longing for dependence on an adult. It might take the form of a great love or attachment for some adult. Nevertheless, we must understand how to observe correctly what is happening in a child at this critical time. A child might suddenly feel isolated and look for something to hold on to. Until now, there was a natural acceptance of authority. Now a child begins to ask, What is this authority? Finding or not finding the right word to say at this moment will make an enormous difference to the child's whole life later on.

When physicians observe childhood illnesses, it is enormously important that they look at the organism in terms of developmental processes that have significance beyond childhood, recognizing that, unless they proceed correctly, the child will suffer its effects in old age. Similarly, we must understand that the ideas, sensations, or will impulses we give children must not be formed in rigid concepts that children must then learn and heed; the ideas, impulses, and sensations that we give them must be as alive as our own limbs. A child's hand is small, and it must be allowed to grow and not constrained. The ideas and soul development of children are also small and delicate, and we must not limit them with hard rules, as though such limits must be retained in the same form thirty years later, once children have grown up. The ideas we bring children must be formed so that they are able to grow.

The Waldorf school is really a preparatory school; every school should prepare children for the great school of adulthood, which is life itself. We must not learn at school for the sake of performance; rather, we must learn at school so that we can learn further from life. This must be the ground of what we might call a spiritual-physiological pedagogy. We must have a feeling for bringing living things to children—things that can continue with them into later life. What we foster in children often lives imperceptibly in the depths of their souls, and in later life it emerges.

We can use an image—it is only an image, but it is based on a truth. There are people who, at a certain time of life, have a beneficial influence on others. They can, if I may use the expression, bestow blessing. Such people do not need to speak but only need to be present with their personality, which blesses. The whole course of a life is usually not seen, otherwise we might notice the upbringing of these people who develop the power of blessing. It may have been a conscious act by just one person, or it may have been unconscious on the part of some teacher. Such people were raised as children to be reverent and, in the most comprehensive sense of the word, to pray, or look up to something. Thus, they could exert their own will toward something. If one has first learned to honor and to be entirely surrounded by authority, then one may be able to bless and become an unquestioned authority.

These things must not live merely as rules for teachers, but must become part of one's being. It must go beyond the head and be digested completely. Thus, one can act through spirit and not merely think thoughts. Such things must come to life in teachers. During the next few days I will describe in detail how this can come about through each year of school, between the ages of seven and fourteen. For the most part, today I wanted to explain how a certain kind of inner life—not merely a view of life but an inner attitude—must become the ground of education.

Once children have outgrown the stage of authority (having reached puberty and a very different relationship to the outer world physiologically), they also gain a very different relationship to the world in soul and body—that is, "bodily life" in its most comprehensive sense. This is the time when the human spirit awakens. Now a person looks for the rational aspect and the logic in all verbal expression. Now we can hope to appeal successfully to the intellect in teaching. It is immensely important that we do not call on the intellect too early, consciously or unconsciously, as people are prone to do today.

Now let's ask ourselves what happens when we see how children accept, on authority, everything that guides their souls. Children do not listen to us and then verify and prove everything we say. Children take in, as an unconscious *inspiration,* all that works on their souls and, through the soul, builds and influences the body. We cannot educate correctly unless we understand this wonderful, unconscious *inspiration* that rules the whole life of children between seven and fourteen—a time when we can work into a continuous process of *inspiration.*

To do this, we must acquire still another power of spiritual cognition. We must add *inspiration* itself to *intuition.* Once we have guided children along as far as the fourteenth year, we make a strange discovery. They begin to find us tedious and tiring whenever we try to present them with something we have conceived logically. Initially, they will listen to our logical formulations, but if they must then rethink our logic, they eventually become weary.

Also during this period, as teachers we need something more than pure logic. We can see this from a general example. Think of a scientist such as Ernst Haeckel, who lived entirely in external nature.[5] He was tremendously interested in all his microscopic studies and all he established. If we teach this to students, they might learn it, but they cannot develop the same interest for it. As teachers, we must develop something different from what children have in themselves. If children are coming into the realm of logic at the age of puberty, we must in turn develop imagery and imagination. Children will be able to hold onto what we give them if we can pour it all into images. Thus they receive images of the world—the activity and meaning of the world—through the pictures we create for them, as in an art form.

So, in this third period of life, we are directed to *imagination,* as in the other two toward *intuition* and *inspiration.* And now we have to look for the spiritual ground that makes it possible for us, as teachers, to work through *imagination, inspiration,* and *intuition*—qualities that enable one to act with spirit, not merely to think of spirit.

This is what I wished to say to you by way of introduction.

---

5. Ernst Haeckel (1834–1919); see *The Riddle of the Universe* (1899).

The Perception of Soul and Spirit

August 17, 1922

I have been informed that something I spoke of yesterday was found difficult to understand—in particular, my use of the terms "spiritual" and "spiritual cognition." Consequently, I will depart somewhat from what I had planned and, instead, speak about these terms, "spirit" (*Geist*) and "spiritual life" (*spirituelles Leben*). This will lead us somewhat away from the subject of teaching and education, but from what I hear, it seems we will better understand one another during the next few days if I explain the concept of spirit, soul, and body. During the next few days I will find an opportunity to say what I had intended to speak of today. Now, a lecture such as today's will require that I speak in a theoretical way, in terms of ideas and concepts. I ask you to consent to this for today, and in the days that follow, things will be better, and I will not torment you cruelly with ideas and concepts but try to please you with concrete facts.

The words *spirit* and *spiritual,* from my present point of view and general outlook, are usually deeply misunderstood. When the word *spirit* is used, people assume it similar to a word like *intellect* or the English word *mind.* But what I mean here is something very different. On the one hand, my meaning must not be confused with the way certain mystical, fanatical, or superstitious sects and movements use the words *spirit* and *spiritual*. On the other hand, it is quite distinct from what is meant by *intellect* or *mind*. We need to understand in a direct, concrete, and real way what is at work in small children, up to the time of the change of teeth. This activity is not directly perceptible, but we see it expressed in a child's nature—which might even appear primitive to us—and thus we can say that this is spirit and soul.

Nowhere in our observations of the human being and nature do we encounter spirit and soul so directly as when we contemplate the manifestations of life in a small child. Here, as I said yesterday, spiritual forces and soul essences are active in the formation of the brain and in the shaping of the whole organism. What we see are manifestations of life in a child; we perceive these with our senses. But it is spirit and soul that work through from behind the veil of sense-perceptible things, so we can apprehend them here as nowhere else in life, unless we have accomplished an inner soul development. Thus we must say that spirit is really unknown to direct, ordinary perception. At most, soul can manifest in ordinary perception, but we must feel and sense it through the percept.

If I may use an image to indicate what is meant (not to explain it), I would say that, when we speak, our speech comes from words—sounds made up of consonants and vowels. Observe the great difference between consonants and vowels in speech. Consonants round off a sound, give it angularity, make it into a breath sound or a wave sound, according to how we form the sound with one organ or another, with lips or teeth. Vowels arise in a very different way. They arise while guiding the breath stream through the vocal organs in a certain way. By means of vowels, we do not give contour but build the substance of a sound. Vowels provide the substance, or content, and consonants mold and sculpt the substance provided by the vowels.

And now, using the words *spirit* and *soul* in the sense we are giving them here, we can say that spirit is in the consonants of speech, and soul is in the vowels.[1] When children first begin to say "ah" (*a*), they are filled with a kind of wonder and marvel—a soul phenomenon. This phenomenon of soul is directly present to us; it flows out in "ah." When children express the sound "eh" (*e*), they exhibit a slight antipathy of soul and withdraw in response to something. "Eh" expresses something antipathetic in the soul. Wonder is expressed by "ah," antipathy by "eh." Vowels reveal soul phenomenon.

When I form any kind of consonant, I surround and shape the vowel sound. When a child says "mama" (a double gesture), it shows a need to reach out to the child's mother for help.[2] By itself, "ah" would express the child's feeling for the mother. "M" expresses what the child would like the mother to do. "Mama" contains the whole relationship between child and mother, in both spirit and soul. Thus we hear language spoken, we hear its meaning, but we fail to notice the way spirit and soul are hidden in language. True, we are occasionally aware of this in speech, but we do not notice it in the whole human being. We see only the outer form of a person, but soul and spirit are within, just as they are within speech. But we no longer notice this.

There was a time in past ages, however, when people did notice this. They did not say, "In the beginning was the Spirit" (which would have been too abstract), but "In the beginning was the word." People still had a living sense of how spirit is carried on the waves of speech. It is this spirit and its nature that we mean when using the word *spiritual*. It is not revealed

---

1. For more on this subject, see Rudolf Steiner, *The Genius of Language* (Anthroposophic Press, 1995) and *Curative Eurythmy* (Rudolf Steiner Press, 1983).
2. The eurythmy gesture "m" is implied.

by intellect, nor by what we call mind. *Mind* and *spirit* are distinct from each other. They differ as much as my person differs from the reflection I see in a mirror. When I hold a mirror and look at myself, my reflection is in the mirror. The reflection moves exactly as I do, and it looks like me, but it is not me. It differs from me because is an image, whereas I am a reality.

Spirit is the reality of hidden depths. Intellect contains only an image of spirit. Mind is a reflected image of spirit. Mind can reveal the activity of spirit, and it can make the motions of spirit, but mind is passive. If someone hits me, mind can reflect it. Mind cannot itself give a blow. Spirit is activity; it is always doing, always creative. Spirit is the essence of productivity—generation itself. Mind, as intellect, is a copy, or reflection and passivity itself—the thing within us that enables us, as adults, to understand the world. If intellect, or mind, were active, we would be unable to comprehend the world. Mind must be passive so that the world can be understood through it. If mind were active, it would continually alter and encroach upon the world. Mind is the passive image of spirit. Thus, we look from the reflection to the person when we seek reality; similarly, when we seek the reality of spirit and soul, we must move from the unproductive and passive to the productive and active.

People have tried to do this throughout all ages of human development. And today, I want to speak to you about one method of this search, so we can agree on the meaning of spirit and soul in what I have to say. Usually, as adult human beings, we perceive spirit only in its reflections as intellect, mind, or reason. We apprehend the soul only in its expressions. We are closer to soul than we are to spirit, but we do not perceive the full inner activity of even the soul. We perceive revelations of the soul, and we perceive spirit only as a reflection. A reflection holds nothing of the reality, but we do perceive revelations of the soul. What we know as feeling—our experience of likes and dislikes, of desire and passion—belongs to the soul. But we do not perceive the nature of soul within us.

What is this soul within? Perhaps I can indicate the nature of soul if I distinguish between our experience and the events that take place within us so that we are able to experience. When we walk over soft ground, our footprints remain. Now suppose a man comes along and discovers our footprints. Will he say that forces in the earth have shaped the earth to form these impressions? No one would say such a thing. Rather, anyone would say, "Someone has walked here."

Materialists say that they find impressions in the brain, just as the earth retains impressions after I have walked on it. But they will say that there are forces in the brain, and these make the impressions. This is not true. The soul makes the impressions, just as I make them on the ground. And it is only because those imprints are there that can I perceive the soul; I perceive a sensation in the soul. At first, the soul is hidden, but it has left its imprints in my body. If I make a very hard dent it causes me pain. Perhaps I do not immediately see what I have done, since it happened behind me. But even when I do not see what I have done, I experience the pain. Similarly, the soul leaves an impression in my body, whereas the soul itself remains hidden. I perceive the effect as passions, sympathy, and so on. I perceive the effect of the soul's activity in the manifestation.

Consequently, with spirit, we have an image; with soul, we have an expression. We are closer to soul, but keep in mind that we must look for spirit or soul more deeply than mind, intellect, or reason. This may help in understanding spirit and soul. And to make the concept of spirit and soul even clearer, let me turn to a historical aspect. And please do not misunderstand me today, as too often happens. I do this simply for the sake of clarification, not with any intention of maintaining that, to reach spirit and soul, we must do as the ancients did.

Nevertheless, the present method of attaining spirit and soul will be easier to understand if we turn to history.

To attain spirit in the twentieth century, it is impossible to proceed as people did hundreds or thousands of years ago in ancient India. Nor can we do as was done before the Mystery of Golgotha.[3] We live within the development of Christianity, but it will help us understand spirit and soul if we look back to this older way and see, for example, how the path to soul and spirit was completely different for those who were spiritual and those who were merely intellectual.

What do we do today when, in keeping with the general consciousness of our age, we want to become clear about ourselves? We reflect by using our intellect. And what do we do when we want to become clear about nature? We experiment, and we bring our intellect to bear upon our experiments. Intellectual activity is everywhere. In ancient times, people tried to reach spirit and soul in a very different way.

I will give two examples from the many I could cite. Aspirants tried to reach spirit and soul in the very ancient East, for instance, through the method of so-called yoga. Today, the mention of yoga produces a feeling of slight horror in many people, since only its later methods are known to history—methods based on human egotism, which seek power in the outer world. The more ancient paths that people took toward the spirit were the older yogic methods, which can be discovered today only through spiritual science, not through conventional science. Those methods were based on their instinctive sense that people could not know spirit through mere reflection, or thinking. They had to do something that would reveal activity in themselves far more than mere reflection could do.

---

3. "The Mystery of Golgotha" is a phrase that Steiner uses to indicate the events surrounding the life of Christ, or the last three years of Jesus' life.

The Perception of Soul and Spirit

Thinking continued, even when they stood aside from the world as mere observers, but it could not bring about any perceptible inner change. Yogis looked for a far more real process within themselves when they wanted to study spirit.

Suppose we ask, in terms of current physiological knowledge, what happens when we use our intellect. An event takes place in our nervous system and brain, as well as in other parts of our organism that are connected with the brain through the nervous system. But this event in the nerves could never happen if an activity far more perceptible were not intermingled with the processes of our brain. Unceasingly, from birth until death, we breathe in, retain our breath, and breathe out. When we breathe in, the breath moves through our whole organism. The thrust of the breath moves through the spinal cord into the brain. We breathe not only with our lungs, but also with our brain. But this means that the brain is in constant motion. As we breathe in, hold the breath, and breathe out, the breath lives and billows within the brain. This goes on continuously, although we are unaware of it today.

A yogi would have said that such events in a human being must become conscious. Thus yogis did not breathe unconsciously in the usual way; they breathed in abnormal ways. They breathed in differently, held the breath differently, and breathed out differently. Through this method, they became conscious of the breathing process. And they experienced with full awareness something that takes place unconsciously for us, because they conceived it and then experienced it. Thus, yogis came to experience how breath unites in the brain with the material process behind thinking and intellectual activity. They looked into this union between thinking and breathing, and they finally experienced the way thought (which, for us, is an abstract thing) pervades the whole body, carried on the tide of breath.

Consequently, thought was not limited to the brain, the lungs, or the heart; thought went into one's very fingertips. From real experience of the breath pulsing through them, yogis learned how spirit creates within a human being through the medium of breath. "And God breathed living breath into the human being, who thus became soul." Not only did God breathe this breath in the beginning, but God breathes continuously wherever breathing takes place. And in the breathing process—not in intellectual process—we become soul. We experience our own being when we feel thought pulsing throughout the body on the tide of breath. Spirit was no longer separated as something intellectual and abstract; hence spirit could be sensed and felt throughout the whole body. One's humanity could be felt as a creation of the gods. They had active spirit.

In intellectuality, spirit is passive, not active. Nowadays, because of our different makeup, we cannot imitate that yoga process, nor would it be proper to do so. What was the goal for yogis? Their goal was to experience how the thinking process is connected with the breathing process. The breath, as their mode of cognition, allowed them to experience their humanity. Yogis united thought more intimately with human nature as a whole than we do today. But our human progress is based on the fact that we have liberated thought and made it far more intellectual than it was when yoga flourished. The discoveries of people like Copernicus, Galileo, Faraday, and Darwin could never have occurred within a system of thought like that of the ancient Indian yogis. Such achievements required a type of thinking that was reduced to reflection, image, and intellectuality. Our whole civilization is based on the fact that we are so different from those who developed yogic philosophy.

People often misunderstand my descriptions of these things. They think that I want to take people back to the philosophy of yoga. This is certainly not the case. On the contrary, I wish to approach matters as they were in the age of Copernicus, Galileo, and Faraday. We must recognize that western civilization achieved its greatness through intellectuality. But our feeling must also be different from that of the ancient Indians; and it must be different, too, from the feeling of those who now practice yoga. Today we must proceed in a way that is quite different from that of ancient Indians; it must be a more spiritual way. Because it must be more spiritual, and because people do not care much for spirit today, it follows that people do not care for the new methods. It is easy, or at least it seems easy, to practice yoga breathing today in an effort to enter the world of spirit. But this is no longer the means whereby people should enter spiritual realms. Rather, modern people must first experience the world of appearance (the unreal image of things), which we can perceive by mere intellectualism. Today, at some point, we must experience the suffering that goes along with the realization that, as long as one is occupied solely with intellectual activity and observations, one lives in emptiness and mere images, remote from reality.

What I am saying seems insignificant, but it is great in terms of inner experience. Once we have the experience that all intellectual thinking is unreal, a mere image, then we experience in our souls something that the body would experience as fainting; we experience fainting in the soul in relation to reality. In fact, knowledge does not begin when you can say, "I think, therefore I can reflect on all things." Rather, knowledge begins when you can say, "Although I think about everything with my image thinking, I am only a weak, impotent being." Yogis looked for their humanity in the breath; today, we must lose our humanity and become weak and faint through our intellectuality. Today, we should be able to say, "I must not go inward through the breathing process, as did the yogis. I must move outward—looking at every flower, every animal, and every human being—and live in the outer environment."

In my book *How to Know Higher Worlds,* I described how to do this—how to look at more than just the outer plant by participating in all its processes, so that thinking is taken out of its image nature to participate in the life of the outer world. Or we can sink into a plant, until we feel gravity going down through the roots into the earth and the formative forces unfolding above. We participate in the unfolding flower and fruit of a plant, diving right into the external world. Thus we are taken up by the external world. We awaken as though from a trance. And now we no longer receive abstract thoughts, but *imaginations*. We get pictures, but a materialistic view would not recognize such images as knowledge. Knowledge, it is said, involves abstract, logical concepts. This is true—but how, if the world is not meant to be comprehended through abstract, logical concepts? If the world is a work of art, we must understand it artistically, not logically. Here, logic is only a means of discipline. We should not understand anything about the world through logic. Consequently, we must enter the objects themselves. Whereas yoga went inward, we must go outward and endeavor in this way to unite with all things. Thus, we can in fact attain the same thing, only in a more soulful and spiritual way. By permeating reality with the discoveries of mere intellectual ideas, we get a renewed sense of how spirit works creatively in us.

And from this, we must begin to feel the reality working in children. It is not the so-called mind in us that is active; in a small child, this would not be creative. This notion would only lead us astray. Rather, in a small child, the active principle is just what we come to know in the creative way described; it is this that forms the second teeth according to the first, concluding in the seventh year.

Nevertheless, we are not called on to do this. A few people in the world can develop such higher knowledge; everyone else needs only sound judgment and observation. Everything these few discover, others can recognize through sound judgment and sound observation. Not everyone, for example, can observe the transits of Venus. These are visible far too rarely, and astronomers can observe them occasionally when they are visible. But does this mean that it would be illogical to speak of the transits of Venus, simply because one had not seen them? After all, the object and method of observation can be understood. It is the same thing with the spiritual world. Simply because of egotism today, people want to do everything themselves. One can argue that, as teachers, we cannot immediately become clairvoyant. We cannot train in such methods. How can we manage teaching if we are first confronted with this complicated method of reaching spirit?

There is another way of making spiritual things fruitful and using them, however. Again, I will illustrate this with an example. Imagine I am teaching a nine- or ten-year-old girl. I want to tell her about the immortality of the human soul. If I go into philosophic dissertations, however charming, this child will make nothing of it at her age. She will remain untouched by my little lecture. But if I say to her, "Dear, see how the butterfly comes out of the chrysalis? There you have an image that you can apply to people. Look at the human body; it is like a butterfly's cocoon. The butterfly flies out of the chrysalis, and in the same way, after death, the soul flies out of the body. Only, the butterfly is visible, and the soul is invisible."

Now I merely suggest this image here. For a child, I would elaborate. Where this has been put in practice, I have found two things: when a teacher describes this image to a child, the child does not understand it. The teacher might convery a charming image, but nothing reaches the soul, and the true object is missed. Another teacher might describe this picture, perhaps in the very same words, and the child will have a real insight as the whole image enters the soul.

Where is the difference? The first teacher is very smart and ingenious, infinitely clever. So the thought arises that a truly intelligent person would not consider the chrysalis and butterfly to be an valid image; we can get away with this only because the child is foolish. One invents a clever image for a silly child; we have a clever teacher and a foolish child, and one who invents a picture for a foolish child will not be understood. You can depend on it; the teacher will not be understood.

Now another teacher believes in this picture. Here a different thought arises—that the divine goodness of the world has itself placed this image into nature so that we may better understand immortality. It is not something we have to invent; rather, we discover the image. The creative spirit of nature makes this image for us so that we may see immortality in its image. God himself painted this picture in nature. If one believes in this image, then a child will believe in it. The child gets all that is needed, simply because one is not thinking, I an clever, the child is foolish. Rather, one thinks of the child as having brought intelligent spirit into the world through birth. The child is intelligent. The child's spirit is not yet awake, and if we are unable to awaken it, it is we who are foolish, not the child.

Once the thought arises in us that children possess hidden intelligence and that we have manifested foolishness, and once we realize that it is our duty to become intelligent by learning from children, then we can make a real impression with our instruction.

In the first case, we have a teacher who thinks of himself or herself as clever, an example of how the intellect works. In the second case, we see an example how spirit works; we see something spiritual and inwardly alive and reaching for the nature of things. This teacher can be effective, even without clairvoyant vision of the spirit. Spirit is active there. You are working in active spirit when you believe in your own pictures. If you do not believe in your image, but make up an image only through intelligence and intellectuality, you remain outside reality with your intellect and mind, with only a mirror image. Mirror images do not act; they are merely passive. Spirit is productive and creative. And it is essential to become creative and to be at home in creating if we wish to be active in spirit.

Thus, through the soul's own work and by working our way into imagination itself, we approach and enter gradually into spirit. First, however, we need to experience the importance of the intellect; then, we enter the spiritual.

This must be the conclusion for today, since it is too late to continue. Tomorrow I will describe another way to spirit, and then continue with our theme. Yesterday's request made it necessary to explain these concepts more exactly. I hope you will accept this as necessary for a proper understanding. Soon, after I have explained this other path—the ascetic path, in contrast to the yoga path—we will be finished with this grim pastime, and then we will be able to go into actual methods of education.

The Spiritual Ground of Physical Education

August 18, 1922

Today I need to add to what I said yesterday about the old ways to spiritual knowledge. Another example of this is the path of self-denial as practiced in previous times, or asceticism in the broadest sense of the term. I will describe a path that is even less practical these days than the one described yesterday. The thoughts and customs of our civilization are different from those when people sought high spiritual knowledge through asceticism. Consequently, just as we need to replace the way of yoga with something more purely spiritual and soulful today, the way of asceticism must also be replaced by a modern path. But we can more easily comprehend the modern path to spiritual life if we focus on understanding the way of asceticism.

Asceticism is essentially a matter of certain exercises, and these may extend to spiritual and soul matters. For now, I would like to deal with the way these exercises were used to eliminate the human body from all of human experience in a particular way and at certain times. This experience of spiritual worlds is invoked only by eliminating the body. Such exercises consisted of training the body through pain, suffering, and mortification, until it could endure pain without disturbing the mind too much, and the ascetic could bear physical suffering without the mind and soul being overwhelmed. Mortification and enhanced endurance were pursued because, as a matter of experience, if the physical was repressed, one's spiritual nature emerged and brought about direct spiritual perception. Although such methods are not to be recommended today, it is a matter of experience that, to the degree the physical body is suppressed, one is able to receive soul and spirit. It is simply a fact that spirit becomes perceptible when physical activity is suppressed.

Let me make myself clear with an example. Think of the human eye. It is there to transmit impressions of light to a human being. What is the only way the eye can make light perceptible? Imaginatively expressed, it does this by wanting nothing for itself. As soon as the eye wants something for itself, so to speak, the eye loses its vitality (perhaps opacity or hardening of the lens or eye occurs); it no longer serves human nature. The eye must claim nothing for its own sake. (This is intended figuratively, of course, but things must be stated in a somewhat concrete way for the sake of expression.) Thus we could say that the eye owes its transparency to the fact that it shuts itself off from the human being and becomes selfless. So, if we want to see into the spiritual world, we must, as it were, make our whole organism into an eye (in a spiritual-soul sense). We must make our whole organism transparent, not physically as do the eyes, but spiritually. The body must no longer be an obstacle to our interaction with the world.

I am not saying that our physical organism, as it exists today, would become diseased (as the eye would be) if it claimed life for its own. In terms of ordinary life, our physical organism is quite all right as it is; it must be opaque. In the lectures that follow, we will see why our organism cannot become an "eye" in ordinary life and why it must not become transparent. Our ordinary soul life can rest in our organism only because it is not transparent—because we are not aware of the whole spiritual world when we look around. So, for ordinary life, it is proper and normal for our organism to be opaque. Nevertheless, we cannot perceive the spiritual world through it, just as we cannot know light through an eye with a cataract. When the body is mortified by suffering and pain and self-denial, it becomes transparent. And just as it is possible to perceive the world of light when the eye lets light flow through it, likewise it is possible for the whole organism to perceive the surrounding spiritual world when we make the organism transparent in this way. What I just described occurred in ancient times and led to the powerful religious visions handed down to us by tradition; they are not the independent discoveries of people today. This is what led to the bodily asceticism I have tried to describe.

Today, we cannot imitate such asceticism. In earlier times it was accepted that, if one sought enlightenment and wished to know the suprasensory spiritual world, one would join solitary individuals and withdraw from life. It was a universal belief that one could learn nothing from those who lived ordinary life in the world. Knowledge of spiritual worlds could be gained only in solitude, and one who sought such knowledge had to become different from others.

It would be impossible to think like this from our modern perspective. We tend to believe only in a person who can stand firmly on two feet—one who can help others and who counts for something in life, one who works and trades and is worldly. The solitude that was considered a prerequisite of higher knowledge in previous ages has no place in our view of life. Today we believe only in a person of action, one who enters life and never retires from it. So it is impossible to acquire an ascetic state of mind in relation to knowledge, and we cannot learn of spiritual worlds in this way.

Because of this, we must approach clairvoyance through soul-spiritual methods, without damaging our bodily fitness through ascetic practices. And we can do this, because we have gained exact ideas through a hundred years of natural scientific development; we can discipline our thinking through natural science. I am not describing something that is antagonistic to the intellect. Intellectuality must be the basis and foundation of clear thinking. And we must build something that can lead to the spiritual world upon the foundation of this intellectuality.

Today people easily meet the requirement to think clearly. This is not intended to belittle clear thinking, but in an age that comes several centuries after Copernicus and Galileo, clear thinking is almost natural. The real pity is that it is not yet natural among the majority. Indeed, it is easy to be clear at the expense of thinking fully; empty thoughts easily become clear. But the foundation of our future development must be clear thinking that is full of meaning.

Now, what the ascetic attained by mortification and by suppressing the physical organism we can attain by taking charge of our own soul development. At some point in life, for example, we can ask ourselves about the sort of habits we have acquired, or about our characteristics, faults, sympathies, or antipathies. And when we have reviewed all this clearly, we can try to imagine (beginning with something simple) what we might be like if a different kind of sympathy or antipathy were developed in the soul.

These things do not arise automatically. It can take years of inner work to do what life would do for us otherwise. If we look honestly at ourselves, we have to admit that we are more than we were ten years ago. The inner form and substance of the soul have become quite different. Now, what has caused this? It is life itself. We have unconsciously surrendered and plunged into the flow of life. And now, can we ourselves do what life would otherwise do? Can we look ahead, for example, to what we might become in ten years, set it as a goal, and then proceed with iron will to make it happen? If we can encompass all life within our own I—the vast life that otherwise affects us—and if we can concentrate within our will the power that is usually spread out as the sea of life, then we can influence our own progress and make something out of ourselves. Thus, within our own being we can achieve the same thing that an ancient ascetic accomplished externally. The ascetic rendered the body weak, and thus the will and cognition would arise from the weakened body, and the body could become translucent to the spiritual world. We must make the will strong and strengthen our thought forces, so that they can become stronger than the body, which goes its own way. Thus we constrain the body to become transparent to the world of spirit. We do the exact opposite of the ascetics of ancient times.

I covered these things in *How to Know Higher Worlds*. What I described there differs completely from the old ascetic way, but many people have confused it with asceticism; they have taken it as the old asceticism in a new form. But anyone who reads it carefully will see that it is different in every way from the asceticism of the past. This new "asceticism" does not require us to withdraw from life and become hermits; rather, it keeps us active in the world, and it is achieved only by looking away from the passing moment to time itself.

Consider, for instance, what you will be like in ten years. This means that you must consider the whole span of human life between birth and death. People tend to live in the moment, but here the goal is to live in time, within the whole span of life. The world of spirit thus becomes visible to us; we do indeed see a spiritual world around us once the body has thus become transparent. For example, everything described in my *Outline of Esoteric Science* is based entirely on such knowledge, which is obtained while the body is as transparent to spirit, just as the eye is transparent to light.

Now you might agree with what I've said but argue that we cannot require such spiritual cognition of everyone before becoming a teacher. As I said about yoga yesterday, let me say again that this is not at all necessary. The child's body itself is a living witness to spiritual worlds, and this is where our higher knowledge can begin. Thus teachers who have right instinct can grow naturally toward treating children in a spiritual way. Our intellectual age, however, has mostly gone away from such a spiritual approach and treats everything rationally. This has happened to the degree that it is said we must educate children—regardless of the stage—to immediately understand what we present. Now this lends itself to triviality, which is no doubt extremely convenient for teachers. We can do quite a bit in a short time if we present children with as many things as possible in a trivial and rudimentary form and address it to their comprehension. But those who think like this, on rational grounds, are not concerned with the whole course of human life. They are unconcerned about what becomes of the sensations teachers have aroused in children once those children have grown into older men and women or reached old age.

Such people do not consider life. For example, they would not consider it significant if I say that children between the change of teeth and puberty should rely mainly on authority, or that to establish trust, they need an example. I might tell a child something that must be taken on trust, since I am the mediator between the divine spiritual world and the child. The child believes me and accepts what I say, but does not yet understand it. We do not understand much of what we receive unconsciously in childhood. If we could accept only what we understood as children, we would receive little of value for later life. And the German poet and thinker Jean Paul [1763–1825] would never have said that more is learned in the first three years of life than in three years at a university.

Just consider what it means when, say, in your thirty-fifth year, some event causes you to feel that something is swimming up into your mind, something heard from a teacher long ago. Perhaps you were only nine or ten at the time and did not understand it at all, and now it comes back. And, in the light of your own life, it now makes sense, and you can appreciate it. If, during later life, you can take something from the depths of your memory and, for the first time, understand it, you have within yourself a wellspring of life; a refreshing stream of power continually flows within you. When something arises in the soul that was once accepted on trust and is only now understood, we can see that to teach properly we must not consider only the immediate moment but the whole of life. In all that we teach children, this must be kept in view.

Now I have just been told that someone took exception to the image I used to show a child how the human being partakes of immortality. I was not speaking of eternity, but of *immortality.* I said that the image of a butterfly emerging from a chrysalis is there to be seen. This image was used to represent only the sensation we can have when the soul leaves the physical body. The image itself refutes this objection; it was used specifically to meet the argument that the emerging butterfly is not the right concept of immortality. In a logical sense, naturally, it is not a right concept. But we are considering the kind of concept we would give children—an image we would place before their souls to avoid confronting them too early with logic. When we present a picture in this way to a child of eight or nine (after all, we are speaking of children, not philosophers) it can grow into the correct idea of immortality.

Thus it all depends on the *what*—on having a lively understanding of existence. It is this that our rationalistic age finds so difficult to understand. It must be obvious to anyone that people speak differently to children than they do to adults. What would be the point of saying that a child is unskilled, immature, and childish if we were in fact talking about an adult? Any observer of life sees not only children and mature youths, but also childish and mature ideas and concepts. As true teachers, it is life itself that we must look to, not adulthood.

It seems to me a good fate that it did not fall to me before 1919 to take on the direction of the Waldorf school, which was founded that year by Emil Molt in Stuttgart. I was concerned professionally with education before then, but I would not have felt able to master (relatively speaking) such a great educational enterprise as we are now able to do with our college of teachers at the Waldorf school. And why is this? Before then, I would never have thought it possible to form such a college of teachers of men and women with such a knowledge of human nature—and thus of child nature—as I was able to do that year. As I said, all true teaching and pedagogy must be based on knowledge of human nature. But before we can do this, we must have a means of penetrating human nature in the proper way. Now, if I may say so, the first perceptions of this understanding of human nature came to me more than thirty-five years ago.

Those were spiritual perceptions of human nature—spiritual, not intellectual. Spiritual truths act in a different way than do intellectual truths. What we perceive intellectually and have proved, as they say, we can also communicate to others, since the matter is ready when logic is. But spiritual truths are not ready when logic is. It is the nature of spiritual truths that they must be carried with us on our way through life—we must live with them before they can develop fully. I would never have dared to tell others certain truths about human nature as they came to me more than thirty-five years ago. I never spoke of these things until I wrote *Riddles of the Soul* a few years ago; thirty years lay between the first idea and presenting these things to the world.[1] Why? Because one needs to contemplate such truths at different stages of life; they must accompany one through various phases. The spiritual truths that one conceived as a young man in his early twenties are experienced quite differently than when he reaches his mid-thirties or forties. And as a matter of fact, it was not until I had passed my fiftieth year that I ventured to publish these outlines of a knowledge of the human being in a book. And only then could I tell these things to a college of teachers, giving them the elements of education that every teacher must claim and use with each and every child.

Thus I may say that, when my little booklet *The Education of the Child in the Light of Anthroposophy* appeared, I spoke of education as one who disagrees with much in modern education—as one who would like to see this or that treated more fundamentally and the like.[2] But when this little book was written, I would not have been able to undertake anything like directing the Waldorf school. It was essential that such a task have a college of teachers who know that the human being originates in a spiritual world. Such knowledge of the human being is very difficult to acquire today; by comparison, natural science is easy to study. It is relatively easy to realize the nature of the final member of organic evolution. We begin with the simplest organism and see how it has evolved up to the human being, who stands at the summit of evolution, the final member of organic development. But we know the human being only as a product of organic development. We do not see directly into the very being of humankind. Natural science has attained a certain perfection, which we greatly admire and do not intend to disparage; but once we have mastered natural science, we know the

---

1. Published as *The Case for Anthroposophy* (Rudolf Steiner Press, 1970).
2. This essay is contained in *The Education of the Child and Early Lectures on Education* (Anthroposophic Press, 1996).

human being as the highest animal, but not the most essential nature of humankind. Yet our life is dominated by this natural science. To educate, we need a practical human science that applies to every individual child, for which we need a general human science.

Today I will indicate a only few of the principles that became apparent to me more than thirty years ago. We have made these the basis for training the staff at the Waldorf school. Now, bear in mind that, when we work with elementary school children (seven to fourteen), we are concerned with the their soul life. In the next few days I will also speak of very small children. But, though it grieves me, we do not yet have a preschool, because we have no money for it, and so we cannot take children until they are six or seven years old. But, naturally, it would be ideal for children to receive education as early as possible.

Once children have passed the age of puberty, they begin an age when we must no longer speak of them as a children. This is the age when young men and women fully acquire their own mind and spirit. Thus human beings progress from the body, by way of the soul, into spirit. As we shall see, however, we cannot teach matters concerning spirit; this must be absorbed freely from the world and from life. When we receive children into elementary school, it is their souls that concern us—that is, their basic physical education has been accomplished or has failed—according to the lights of parents and educators. Thus we can say that the most essential aspect of physical education belongs to the period ending with the change of teeth, though it is continuous, of course, as we shall see when I describe the particular phases of education. From that time on, it is the children's souls that we must work with, and we must direct their development in a way that also strengthens their physical development.

When we have elementary school children, we must deal with the soul, which manifests more or less through thinking, feeling, and willing. If we can thoroughly understand the soul life of thought, feeling, and volition within the whole human being, we have the basis for all of education.

To be sure, the multiplication table is only a part of mathematics, but we must learn it before we can advance to differential and integral calculus. In education, things are a little different. It is not a wonderfully advanced science that I am about to present, but only the basics. In this case, however, advanced science cannot be built as we would differential and integral calculus on elementary mathematics; teachers must base it on a practical use of these basic principles.

In today's materialistic age, people speak of the nature of the human soul—when they acknowledge the existence of the soul at all—and one even hears of a psychology, or science, of the soul, though it is completely without soul. And those who allow the existence of the soul usually say that, today, it is experienced inwardly and intuitively and that the soul is connected in some way with the body (though I will not get into the philosophical aspect of this). Indeed, when we survey the field of our exceptionally intelligent psychology, we find that it connects the whole soul—thought, feeling, and volition—to the human nervous system in the broadest sense. Accordingly, it is the nervous system that brings the soul to physical manifestation and serves as the material foundation for the soul's life.

This is what I recognized as an error thirty-five years ago. The only part of our soul life as adults—I emphasize *adults*, since we cannot consider the child until we understand the adult—the only part of our soul life that is connected with the nervous system is our thinking, or power of ideation. The nervous system is connected only with ideation.

Human feeling is not related directly to the nervous system, but to what we might call the "rhythmic" system. It involves the marvelous interrelationship between breathing and the blood's circulation. Their ratio is only approximate, since it naturally varies from person to person. In general, however, every adult has four times as many pulse beats as breaths. This internal interplay of pulsing and breathing rhythms is in turn related to the more extended rhythms of human life and constitutes our rhythmic nature—a second nature, in contrast to the head, or nerve, nature. Our rhythmic system includes the rhythmic experience of sleeping and waking. We often make this pattern nonrhythmic today, but it is a rhythm, and there are many other rhythms in human life. Our life is not built only on the life of the nervous system; it is based also on the rhythmic life. Just as thinking and the forces of thought are related to the nervous system, the power of feeling is directly related to our rhythmic system.

Feeling is not expressed directly in the nervous system but in the rhythmic system. Once we begin to conceive of our rhythmic system and make concepts of our feelings, we can perceive our feelings as ideas by means of the nerves, just as we perceive light or color externally. Thus the connection between feeling and the nerveous system is indirect; its direct connection is with the rhythmic system. You simply can't understand the human being unless you know we breathe and how this is related to blood circulation.

You must understand how this rhythm appears, for example, when a child quickly blushes or grows pale; you must understand everything related the rhythmic system. On the other hand, you must also know the processes that accompany children's passions—their loves and affections. If you cannot form an idea of what lives directly in the life of rhythm and how this is merely projected into the life of nerves, you do not know the human being. You do not understand the human being if you think that the soul's nature depends on the nerveous system and is merely thinking, which depends on the nerves.

What I am talking about arises from direct observation, such as one makes through spiritual perception. There is no proof of the validity of this spiritual observation, as one can prove the findings of intellectual thinking. But anyone who considers these views without bias will be able prove them retrospectively through normal human understanding and, moreover, through the findings of natural science on these matters. I might add that thirty-five years ago, I was involved in verifying the original concept of how human nature is made up of various members, which I am speaking of now. Much of the work I had to do involved investigating the domains of physiology, biology, and other natural sciences to discover whether these things could be verified externally. I would not speak of these things today if I had not received this support. In general, it can be stated with certainty that much of what I am saying now can be demonstrated by modern scientific means.

Now, in the third place, in contrast to thinking and feeling, we have volition, or our life of will. Volition does not depend directly on the nervous system but relates directly to human metabolism and movement; metabolism is very intimately connected with movement. You can regard all human metabolism, in addition to movement itself, to be the limb system. I consider the third member of the human organism to be the movement and metabolic system, and volition is immediately related to this. Every human will impulse is accompanied by a form of metabolic process, whose mode of operation is different from that of the nerve processes that accompany thinking. Of course, people need a healthy metabolism for a sound process of thinking. Thinking is related directly to the activity of our nervous system, which is very different from metabolic activity, while human volition is directly connected with metabolism. We must recognize this dependence of volition on the metabolism.

When we think and develop ideas about our own volition, metabolic activity is thus projected into the nervous system. Volition works only indirectly in the nervous system. Events in the nervous system that are related to volition are the faculty of apprehending our own will activity. Thus, when we penetrate the human being with vision, we discover the relationships between human soul and physical nature. The activity of thought in the soul manifests physically as nervous activity. Feeling nature in the soul manifests physically as the rhythms of breathing and blood circulation. It does this directly, not indirectly through the nervous system. Active volition manifests in physical human nature as a subtle metabolism. It is essential to recognize the fine metabolic processes that accompany the exercise of volition; it is a kind of combustion in the human being.

Today, I can give you only a general outline of these things, but as you acquire these concepts, their details will become clear in the next few days. I will describe their application, and once you have the elementary principles, your eyes will also be opened to everything that you encounter in the nature of children. In children, things are not yet reached the states described. As I explained, for example, a child is entirely a sense organ, specifically, all head.

It is particularly interesting to use scientific spiritual observation to see how a child tastes in a different way than does an adult. Adults have brought taste into the realm of consciousness; they taste something with the tongue and decide what that taste is. A baby, during the earliest weeks, tastes with the whole body, because the organ of taste is diffused throughout the organism. A baby tastes with the stomach and continues to taste as the nourishing juices are absorbed in the lymph system and transmitted throughout the organism. When babies nurse, they are completely permeated by taste. And here we see how the child is, so to speak, illuminated and transfused with taste, with something of a soul nature. Later on, we no longer have this in our body as a whole, but only in our head.

Thus we learn how to watch a tiny child and how to watch an older child, knowing that one child will blush easily for one reason or another, and another will easily turn pale; one is quick to get excited or moves the arms and legs quickly; one child walks firmly, while another walks lightly. Once we have these principles and recognize that the soul's expression of volition is seated in the metabolic system; that the expression of feeling rests in the rhythmic system; that what manifests in the soul as thought is based in the nervous system, then we will know how to observe children; we will know where to look.

You all know that there are those who use a microscope to investigate certain things. They see wonderful things in this way. There are also people who have not learned how to look through a microscope; they look into it, and no matter how they manipulate it they see nothing. First one must learn to see by learning how to manipulate the instrument through which one sees. Once a person has learned how to look through a microscope, one is able to see what is needed. People see nothing of the human being until they have learned to see with the soul and spirit all that corresponds to thinking, feeling, and volition. The goal of the Waldorf school has been to develop the correct orientation of vision in the staff. Teachers must first know what goes on in children, then they can achieve the right state of mind, and the right education comes only from the right mental attitude.

It was necessary to begin with an account of the threefold human organization so that you will more readily understand the details of practical educational methods.

The Art of Educating Young Children

August 19, 1922

It might seem as though the art of education as described in these lectures would lead away from practical life into some remote, purely spiritual region, as though this kind of education stressed the purely spiritual domain too much. From what I have said so far in describing the spiritual foundation of the education, this might appear to be the case. But it only seems this way. In reality, the art of education that arises from this philosophy has the most practical objectives. Thus, it should be realized that the main reason for speaking of spiritual facts here is to answer the educational question, How can we best develop the physical organism of children and youths?

It may look like a fundamental contradiction when a spiritual philosophy considers the development of the physical organism first. My theme during the next few days, however, will do more toward dispelling this contradiction than any abstract statements I could make at the beginning. Today, I would just like to say that anyone who speaks on questions of education today is put in a peculiar situation. If one sees much in education that needs reforming, it is like expressing a dissatisfaction with one's own education. It implies that one's own education has been very poor. And one presumes to know the right way to educate, even as the product of this very bad education in which there is so much to criticize. Otherwise why be a reformer? This is the first contradiction. The second gives one a slight feeling of shame when facing an audience and speaking on education; for one is speaking of what education should be and how it must be changed from present practice. It amounts to saying that you are all badly educated. And yet one appeals to those who are badly educated so that we can bring about a better education. One assumes that both the speaker and the audience know very well what good education should be—despite the fact that they have been very badly educated.

Now this is a contradiction, but it is one that life presents us, and in fact it can be solved only through the kind of education being described here. One can thoroughly recognize the problems with education and where it needs improvement, just as you can see that a picture is painted well without having the slightest capacity for painting yourself. You can consider yourself able to appreciate the merits of a picture by Raphael without thinking you can paint such a picture. In fact, it would be a good thing today if people would think like this. But they are not content with merely knowing; where education is concerned, people claim immediately to know how to educate. It is like someone who is not a painter and could never become a painter, but who nevertheless sets out to show how a badly painted picture should have been painted.

The assertion here is that it's not enough to know what good education is; rather, one must have a grasp of the technique and detail of education as an art, and one must gain practical skill. Knowledge and understanding are needed for this. Thus, yesterday I tried to explain the basic principles for guidance in this ability, and now I will continue this review.

It is easy to say that we develop during our lifetime, and that we develop in successive stages. But this is not enough. Yesterday we saw that the human being is threefold in nature, that human thinking is physically connected with the nervous system; feeling is related to the rhythmic system, particularly the breathing and circulation system; and that volition is related to the system of movement and metabolism.

The development of these three human systems varies. Through the various phases of life, they develop in different ways. During the first, until the change of teeth (as I have repeatedly stated), children are all sense organ and head, and all development proceeds from the nervous system. This system permeates the whole organism, and all outer impressions affect the organism as a whole, working right through it, just as light affects the eye later in life. In other words, in an adult, light comes to a standstill in the eye, and sends only an idea of itself, a concept of light, into the organism. In children, it's as though every little blood corpuscle were inwardly illumined and transfused with light (to give it a somewhat exaggerated and pictorial expression). At this stage, children are entirely exposed to these etheric essences, which in later life we arrest in the sense organs at the surface of our bodies, while inwardly we develop something entirely different. Thus, children are exposed far more to sensory impressions than adults are.

Observe a concrete example of this. Imagine a man who has charge of nurturing of a very young child—perhaps a tiny baby. He is a person with his own world of inner experience. Imagine that this person is a heavyhearted being, one to whom life has brought sorrow. In the mature man, the physical consequences of those experiences will not be obvious, having left only faint traces. When we are sad, the mouth is always a little dry. And when sadness becomes a habit and a continuous state, the sorrowful person goes about with dry mouth, a dry tongue, a bitter taste in the mouth, and even a chronic inflammation of the mucous membrane. In adults, these physical conditions are merely faint undertones of life.

A child growing up in the company of an adult is an imitator. Children model themselves entirely on what they perceive in the appearance of the adult—for example, an adult's sad way of speaking or sad feelings. There is a subtle interplay of imponderables between children and adults. When we experience inner sadness with all its physical manifestations, a child, being an imitator, takes up these physical effects through inner gestures. Through inward mimicry, a child might assume, say, a dry tongue, or bitter taste, in the mouth, and this (as I pointed out yesterday) flows through the whole organism. Or a child absorbs the pale, sad face of an adult. Children cannot imitate the soul substance of sorrow itself, but they do imitate the physical appearance of the sorrow. Consequently, because spirit is still working into a child's organism, the whole organism will be permeated in such a way that it builds the organs according to the physical manifestations the child has taken in. Thus, the very condition of the growing organism will make a sad being of the child. In later life, this person will have a particular aptitude for perceiving anything sad or sorrowful. Such is the subtle, delicate knowledge one needs to educate properly.

This is the way of life for children until the change of teeth. They are entirely surrendered to what the organism has absorbed from adults around them. And the inner conflict here is perceptible only to spiritual science; this struggle can be described only as a fight between inherited characteristics and adaptation to environment. We are born with certain inherited characteristics, and this can be seen by anyone who has the opportunity to observe a child during the earliest weeks and years. Science has produced an extensive body of knowledge on this subject. But children have to adapt more and more to the world. Little by little, they must transform their inherited characteristics until they do not merely carry their heredity, but open their senses, soul, and spirit to receive the events of the greater environment. Otherwise they become egotistic people who want only what agrees with the inherited characteristics.

Now we have to educate people to be receptive to all that goes on in the world, so that, whenever they see something new, they can bring their judgment and feelings to meet it. We must not educate people to be self-absorbed; rather, we must educate people to meet the world with free and open minds, to act in harmony with all that the world requires. This attitude is a natural outcome of the approach I described yesterday. Thus we must closely observe the inner struggle that takes place during children's early years, between heredity and adaptation to the environment. Try to study with the greatest human devotion the wonderful process in which the first teeth are replaced by the second. The first teeth are inherited; they seem almost unsuitable for the outer world. Gradually, above each inherited tooth, another tooth forms. In shaping each tooth, the form of the first is used, but the form of the second, permanent tooth is adapted to the world.

I always refer to this process of changing teeth as characteristic of this particular period of life, up to the seventh year. But it is only one indication; what happens to the teeth is conspicuous, because teeth are hard organs, but the process takes place throughout the organism. When we are born into this world, we carry within us an inherited organism. During the first seven years of life, we form a new organism over it. The whole process is physical. But although it is physical, it is the work of spirit and soul within a child. And those of us who are close to children must try to guide them in soul and spirit, so that their inner being goes with, rather than against, the health of the organism. We must therefore know what spirit and soul processes are needed for a child to form a healthy organism to replace the inherited organism. We must be able to understand and work spiritually to promote the physical.

Now, to continue from what I said by way of introduction today, we come to something else. Suppose, as teachers, we are entering a classroom. We must never imagine that we are the most intelligent people, at the summit of human intelligence; this, in fact, would show that we are very poor teachers. Rather, we should think of ourselves as only relatively intelligent. This is a more realistic mind-set than the other. Now, in this state of consciousness, we enter the classroom. As we enter, we must remember that, among these children, there may be a very intelligent being, one who in later life will be far more intelligent than we. Now if we, who are only relatively intelligent, were to bring up this child to be only as intelligent as ourselves, we would render him merely a copy of ourselves. This would be quite wrong. The correct approach would be to educate this very intelligent individual to grow and become far more intelligent than we could ever be. This means that there is something in a person that we must not touch, something we must approach with sensitive reverence, if we are to exercise the art of education properly. This is part of the answer to the question I asked.

Often, in early life, we know very well what we should do, but we cannot carry it out; we feel inadequate. The obstacle that prevents us from doing what we should is usually very obscure, but it is always a condition of the physical organism. For example, it may be a disposition toward sadness acquired through imitation, such as I spoke of. The organism incorporated this tendency, and it has become a habit. Now we want to do something that does not suit an organism inclined toward sadness. Within us, we have the effects of the dry tongue and bitter taste from childhood, and now we want to do something different and we experience difficulty.

If we realize the full significance of this, we might tell ourselves that a teacher's primary task is to nurture the body to be as healthy as possible. This means that we use every spiritual measure to ensure that in later life a person's body will be the least possible hindrance to the will of one's spirit. If we make this our purpose in school, we can develop the forces that lead to an education for freedom.

The extent to which spiritual education has a healthy effect on the physical organism, and on the person as a whole, becomes especially obvious when the vast range of facts given by our modern natural science is gathered and coordinated as only spiritual science can do. Thus we can see how to work in the spirit of the healing the human being. Take a particular instance. The English doctor Sir Clifford Allbutt (1836–1925) made a very significant statement about how human grief and sadness affect the development of the digestive organs, the kidneys in particular. After awhile, people who experience a great many problems and grief in life show signs of malformed kidneys. This has been very finely demonstrated by Dr. Allbutt and is a discovery of natural science.

The important thing is that we know how to use a scientific discovery like this in educational practice. As teachers, we must recognize that, to the degree that we allow children to imitate our own sorrow and grief, our bearing greatly damages their digestive system. You see, this is the tragedy of this materialistic age; many physical facts are discovered, but the relationships are missing. It is this materialistic science that fails to perceive the true significance of the physical and material. The contribution of spiritual science is to show, in every case, how spirit works and its effects in the physical realm. Then, instead of indulging in dreamy mysticism that yearns for castles in the clouds, it follows spirit in every detail and activity. We are spiritual beings only when we recognize spirit as creator—the agent that works on and shapes the material world. It is not the worship of some abstract spirit in the clouds—like mysticism, which, in general, considers matter to be merely a concern of the material world.

Hence, in young children, until the seventh year, we are concerned with recognizing the pervasive interplay of sensory and nerve activity, the rhythmic activity of breathing and circulation, and the activity of movement and metabolism. And it is the nerve and sensory activity that predominates and has the upper hand; thus sensory activity in children always affects their breathing. If they have to look at a face furrowed by grief, it affects their senses first, then their breathing and, in turn, their whole movement and metabolic system.

In children after the change of teeth around the seventh year, we find that the nervous system no longer dominates; it has become more separate and is turned more toward the outer world. In these children, until puberty, it is the rhythmic system that dominates and takes the upper hand. It is most important to keep this in mind during elementary school, when we have children between the change of teeth and puberty. Hence, we must see that it is essential to work with the rhythmic system, and that anything affecting the other systems is wrong. But what affects the rhythmic system? It is affected by art—anything conveyed in an artistic form.

Just think of how everything musical is related to the rhythmic system. Music is nothing but rhythm carried into the human rhythmic system. The inner human being becomes a lyre or violin. One's whole rhythmic system reproduces what the violin or piano has played. And, as it is with music, so it is in a finer, more delicate way with modeling and painting. Color harmonies and melodies are also reproduced and live as inner rhythmic processes within us. Before our teaching can become truly educational, we must know that everything children are taught throughout this period must be conveyed artistically. According to Waldorf principles, the first consideration in the elementary school means composing all lessons in a way that appeals to the rhythmic system of children.

There is little regard for this today. We see this in the continually accumulating scientific observations that completely contradict this appeal to the rhythmic system. Research in experimental psychology attempts to determine how quickly children tire of one activity or another, and then instructors are supposed to take this into account. This is all very well as long as we do not think spiritually. But if we do, the matter appears in a very different light. Experiments can still be made, and they are very good; nothing is said here against the excellence of natural science. But we say that, if children between the change of teeth and puberty show a certain amount of fatigue, you have not appealed in the right way to the rhythmic system, but to some other system. Throughout life, the rhythmic system never tires; the heart beats night and day. Instead, fatigue affects the intellect and the metabolism. When we know that we must appeal to the rhythmic system, we know that we must work artistically. Experiments on fatigue show where we have gone wrong, where we have given too little attention to the rhythmic system. When we discover that a child has become overly fatigued, we must ask ourselves how we can plan our lessons to avoid this. We do not set ourselves up to condemn modernity, claiming that natural science is bad and must be opposed. Spiritual people have no such intention. Rather, they will say that we need a higher view, because this is precisely what allows us to apply natural scientific results to life.

If we now turn to the moral aspect, we must find the best way to encourage children to develop moral impulses. Here we are concerned with the most important of all educational issues. We do not endow children with moral impulses by giving them commands, saying that they must do this or that, or such and such is good. We do not do this by trying to prove that something is good and must be done, or by saying that something is wicked and must not be done. Children do not yet have the intellectual attitude of adults toward good and evil and the whole realm of morality; they must grow into it. This arises only with puberty, after the rhythmic system has accomplished its basic task, when the intellectual forces are ripe for complete development. Then a person may experience the satisfaction of moral discernment in life itself. We must not force moral judgment on children; we merely lay the foundation so that, when children awaken at puberty, they can form their own moral judgments by observing life.

The least effective way to attain this is by giving children finite commands. Rather, we work through examples or by presenting images to their imagination—say, through biographies or descriptions of good or bad people; or by inventing circumstances that present a picture of goodness to their mind. Because the rhythmic system is especially active in children during this period, pleasure and displeasure can arise in them, but not judgment of good and evil. They can experience sympathy with what is good in an image, or a feeling of antipathy toward the evil seen in an image. It is not a matter of appealing to children's intellect by saying, "Thou shalt...." or "Thou shalt not...." It is rather a matter of nurturing esthetic judgment, so that children begin to feel pleasure and sympathy when they see goodness and feel dislike and antipathy when they see evil. This is very different from working on the intellect through precepts formed by the intellect.

Children will not be awake to intellectual precepts until they are no longer ours to educate—when they become adults and learn from life itself. We should not rob them of the satisfaction of awaking to morality on their own. And we will not do this if we prepare them properly during the rhythmic period of their life. Working through imagery, we must train them to take an esthetic pleasure in goodness and feel an esthetic dislike of evil. Otherwise, when children do awake after puberty, they will experience an inward bondage—perhaps not consciously, but throughout life they will lack the important experience of moral discernment awakening and developing within. Abstract moral instruction will not accomplish this awakening; it must be prepared by working correctly in this way in children.

Thus it is always a matter of *how* something is done. We see this both in the part of life concerned with the outer world and in the part concerned with morality—when we study the realm of nature in the most appropriate way, and when we know the best way to plant morals in the rhythmic system of breathing and blood circulation. Once we know how to enter with spirit into the physical, and once we begin to see how spirit weaves continuously in the physical, we will be able to educate in the right way.

Although knowledge of the human being is sought in the first instance for the art of education, nevertheless, in practice the effect of such a spiritual view on the teacher's state of mind has tremendous importance. This can be shown best in relation to the attitude of many of our contemporaries.

No doubt, every age has its shadow side, and there is much in the past that we have no wish to revive. Nevertheless, anyone who can look at human history with a certain intuition will perceive that in our time there are many who have very little inner joy. On the contrary, people are burdened by heavy doubts and questions in terms of destiny. This age has less capacity than any other for deriving its answers from the universe as a whole. Although I might become very unhappy in myself, and with good reason, yet it is always possible to find something in the universe to counter my unhappiness. But modern humankind lacks the strength to find consolation in a universal view as long as personal situations make people downcast. Why is this? It is because the education and development of people today provide little opportunity to gain a feeling of gratitude—gratitude that we are alive at all as human beings in this universe.

Correctly speaking, all human feelings should function from a fundamental sense of gratitude that the cosmos has given us birth and a place within the universe. Any philosophy that ends with abstract observations and fails to flow out in gratitude toward the universe is an incomplete philosophy. The final chapter of every philosophy—its effect on human feeling—should be gratitude toward the cosmic powers. This feeling is essential in teachers and should be instinctive in anyone entrusted with nurturing a child. Therefore, the first important thing to be worked for in spiritual knowledge is thankfulness that the universe has given a child into our keeping.

In this sense, we should never be cut off from reverence and thankfulness for children. We need only one attitude toward children to educate and nurture them correctly: an attitude of reverence, no more and no less. We feel reverence toward many things; a meadow flower can make us feel reverence when we view it as a creation of the cosmic divine spiritual order. Flashing lightning in the clouds make us feel reverence if we can see it in terms of the world's divine spiritual order. And above all, we should feel reverence toward children, because they come to us from the depths of the universe as the highest manifestation of its nature; they bring tidings of the world's essence. Within this feeling, we find one of the most important impulses of educational method. This educational method has a different quality from methods devoted to nonspiritual matters. Educational technique is essentially a moral impulse of reverence in teachers.

Now you may say that, although people are extremely objective toward many things today—things of less vital importance perhaps—we will nevertheless find those who consider it a tragedy that they should feel religious toward a child who may turn out to be completely useless and ineffectual. And why should we consider it a tragedy if a child turns out unsuccessful? As we said before, there are many parents, even in our age of objectivity, who admit that their children are completely useless.

This was not true in former times, when all children were good in their parents' eyes. This was a healthier attitude than the modern one. Nevertheless, we feel it is a tragedy if the spirit worlds give us the gift of a difficult child as a manifestation of the highest. But we must live through this feeling of tragedy, because it is this very feeling that will help us over the rocks and crags of education. If we can feel gratitude even for a difficult child and also feel the tragedy of it, and if we can rouse ourselves to overcome this feeling of tragedy, then we will be in a position to feel gratitude to the divine world. For we must learn to perceive how something "bad" can also be something divine, although this is a very complicated matter. Gratitude must permeate teachers of children up to the change of teeth; it must be their fundamental mood.

Then we come to the part of a child's development based primarily on the rhythmic system. As we have seen, here we must work artistically in teaching. And we shall never accomplish this unless we can join an attitude of reverence toward the child with a love of our educational activity; we must saturate our teaching with love. While children are between the change of teeth and puberty, all our teaching must be done out of love for teaching itself, otherwise it will have no good effect on them. We must tell ourselves that, no matter how clever a teacher may be, the lives of children reveal infinitely significant spiritual divine matters. But, for our part, our love must surround our spiritual efforts toward children in education. Consequently, no pedagogy should be purely intellectual; the only guidance we should engage is that which helps us teach with loving enthusiasm.

In a Waldorf school, *who* the teachers are is far more important than any technical ability they may have acquired intellectually. It is important that teachers not only love the children, but also love the whole procedure they use. It is not enough for teachers to love the children; they must also love teaching, and love it with objectivity. This constitutes the spiritual foundation of spiritual, moral, and physical education. If we can acquire this love for teaching, we will be able to develop children up to the age of puberty so that, when that time arrives, we will be able to hand them over to the freedom and the use of their own intelligence.

If we have received children in religious reverence, and if we have educated them in love up to the time of puberty, then after this we will be able to leave their spirit free and interact with them as equals. Our aim is not to touch the spirit, but to let it awaken. When children reach puberty, we will best attain our goal of giving them over to freely use their intellectual and spiritual powers if we respect the spirit. We must realize that all we can do is remove hindrances from the spirit—physical hindrances and, up to a point, hindrances of the soul. What the spirit must learn, it will learn because you have removed the impediments. If we remove impediments. spirit will develop in relation to life itself, even in very early youth. Our proper task as educators is to remove hindrances.

Hence, we must make sure we do not try to turn out children who are copies of ourselves, and that we do not forcibly and tyrannically impose ourselves on those who will naturally develop beyond us. Each child in every age brings something new into the world from divine regions, and it is our task as educators to remove the bodily and soul obstacles, so that the child's spirit may enter with full freedom into life. These must become the three golden rules in the art of education; they must imbue the whole attitude of teachers and the whole impulse of their work. The golden rules that must be embraced by a teacher's whole being, not as theory, are these: first, reverent gratitude toward the world for the child we contemplate every day, for every child presents a problem given us by divine worlds; second, gratitude to the universe and love for what we have to do with a child; and third, respect for the child's freedom, which we must not endanger, since it is this freedom to which we must direct our teaching efforts, so that the child may one day stand at our side in freedom in the world.

The Art of Educating Older Boys and Girls

August 21, 1922

The change of teeth in a child is a gradual process, and even more gradual is the great transformation in the body, soul, and spirit, which I have already mentioned. Thus, in education it is important to remember that children gradually change from imitative beings into those who look to the authority of an educator. Consequently, we should not make an abrupt transition in the way we treat children around their seventh year, the age when we receive them into elementary school. Anything else said about elementary education must be understood in the light of this principle.

In the art of education with which we are concerned, it is important to foster the development of a child's inherent capacities. Thus, all teaching must be at the service of education. Strictly speaking, the task is to educate, and teaching is used as a means of educating. This educational principle requires that children develop the appropriate relationship to life at the right age. This can be achieved only if we do not begin by requiring children to act against their nature. For example, it is thoroughly unnatural to require children in the sixth or seventh year to simply copy the signs we use in this advanced stage of civilization for reading and writing. If you consider the letters we use for reading and writing, you will

The Art of Educating Older Boys and Girls

realize that there is no connection between these letters and what seven-year-old children do naturally. Keep in mind that when people first began to write they used painted or drawn signs, and these copied objects or events in the environment. People also wrote from will impulses, so that the forms of writing expressed processes of the will; cuneiform is an example.[1]

The completely abstract forms of letters that the eye must look at today arose from picture writing. If we confront young children with these letters, we present them with something alien that in no way suits their nature. Let us be clear about what it really means to force something foreign into a child's organism. It is as though we accustomed children from the earliest years to wearing clothes that are too small—clothes that do not fit and thus damage the organism. Today observation tends to be superficial, and people fail to perceive the damage done to the organism merely by introducing reading and writing to children in a wrong way. An art of education based on knowledge of the human being proceeds truly by drawing out all that is in the child. It does not merely claim that an individual must be developed; it accomplishes this. And this is achieved, first, by not beginning with reading. With children, movements, gestures, and expressions of volition come first, not perception or observation. These come later. So we need to begin not with reading but with writing. But this writing is the kind that will come naturally from the whole human being.

Thus, we begin with writing lessons, not reading lessons, by leading into writing through what children do naturally through imitation, through volition, through the hands. Let me make this clear through an example.

---

1. Cuneiform is composed of slim triangular or wedge-shaped elements, as the characters used in writing by the ancient Akkadians, Assyrians, Babylonians, Persians, and others.

Suppose we ask a child to say the word *fish,* for example, and while doing so, show her the form of the fish in a simple sketch. Then ask her to copy it, and in this way we get the child to experience the word *fish.* From *fish* we go to *f,* and from the form of the fish we can gradually evolve the letter *f.* Thus we derive the form of the letter through an artistic activity that carries what is observed into the will. In this way, we avoid introducing an utterly alien *f,* something that would affect the child like a demon, as though something foreign were thrust into her body. Instead we evoke something she has seen for herself in the grocery store. And we transform this little by little into *f.*

This is how we can approach the way writing originated, since the way it arose is similar to this. But there is no need for teachers to study antiquity and reproduce the way picture writing arose, so that it can be given in the same way to children. It is necessary, however, to use living fantasy and to produce something fresh that leads from the object and immediate life to the letters. You will then find the most varied ways for deriving the letters for children from life itself. For example, while you say "mmm," let children feel how the sound vibrates on the lips, then get them to see the shape of the lips as a form. Then you will be able to go gradually from the "mmm" vibrating on the lips to the letter *m.*

In this way, if you proceed spiritually and imaginatively, not intellectually, you will gradually derive from the children's own activity everything needed to lead them to learn to write. They will learn to write later and more slowly than children usually do today. Parents may worry that their children are eight or nine years old and still do not yet write properly. And we must always let them know that when children learn more slowly at any given age, the material is absorbed in a more certain and healthy way by the organism than if it is forced into them.

Moreover, there is room for the individuality of teachers, and this is an important consideration. Because we now have so many children in the Waldorf school, we have had to begin parallel classes; thus we have two first classes, or grades, two second classes, and so on. If you go into one of the first classes, you will see writing taught through painting and drawing; you can see how teachers are doing this. For example, it might be done just as described here. Then you go into the other first class, and you will find the same subject being taught. But you will see something very different; this teacher allows the children to run round in a kind of eurythmy, getting them to experience the form through their bodily movements. The shape that the child runs in is retained as the form of the letter. And it is possible to do this in a third or a fourth way. You will find the same subject taught in extremely varied ways in different parallel classes. Why? Because it is not a matter of indifference that a teacher has a certain temperament. The lesson will be harmonious only when there is the right contact between a teacher and the whole class. Thus every teacher must present lessons as an individual. Just as life appears in manifold variety, so, too, teaching based on life will take various forms.

Usually, when educational principles are established, they are expected to be carried out. They are written down in a book, and a good teacher is expected to do them exactly, 1 - 2 - 3. I am convinced that if a dozen people (or even fewer) sit down together, they can produce the most wonderful program for education—first, second, third, and so on. People are so wonderfully intelligent these days (and I am not being sarcastic but really mean it); they can think out the most wonderful things in the abstract. But whether they can be put into practice is another matter; this is a concern of life.

When we have to deal with life, isn't life is in all of you—natural life? You are all human beings, but you all look different. No one's hair is like that of another. Life displays variety in manifold forms. Each person has a different face. If you lay down abstract principles, you expect to find the same activities in every classroom. If your principles are taken from life, you know that life is varied and that the same thing can be done in very different ways. You can see, for example, that negroes are also regarded as human beings, yet in them the human form appears quite differently. In the same way, when the art of education is held as a living art, all slavish attention to rules and every sort of formalism must be avoided. Education will become real when it is made into an true art and when teachers become artists. It is possible for us in Waldorf education to teach writing through art. Reading can be learned later, almost naturally and without effort. It comes later than is usual, but it comes almost on its own.

While we are concerned with bringing the pictorial element to children (during the next few days I will show you some of the paintings from Waldorf school), we must also make sure that music is appreciated as early as possible. The musical element provides a good foundation for a strong, energetic will, especially, at this age, if we emphasize not so much musical content as the rhythm and beat of the music. This is especially so if it is treated in the right way at the beginning of elementary school. I said in the introduction to the eurythmy performance that we should introduce eurythmy into children's education.[2] I will say more in a later lecture about eurythmy, particularly as

---

2. The performance took place August 18 at this conference. Steiner's introduction is in *An Introduction to Eurythmy* (Anthroposophic Press, 1984).

it relates to education. For the moment, I wanted to give one or two more examples of how early instruction serves education, insofar as it is called from the nature of the human being.

We must keep in mind that, during the first part of the phase between the change of teeth and puberty, children cannot distinguish between what is inwardly human and what is external. Until the eighth or ninth year, these two aspects are still united. Inwardly, children feel a certain impression, while outwardly they may see a certain phenomenon—for example, a sunrise. They project the forces they feel inside when unhappy or suffering pain into the sun or moon, or a tree or plant. And we should not reason children out of this feeling; rather, we must transport ourselves into their stage of life and do everything in education as if no boundary existed yet between one's inner being and outer nature. We can do this only when we teach with as much imagination as possible, allowing plants to act in a human way by speaking with one another and so on; we introduce humanity everywhere. People today have a horror of so-called anthropomorphism. But children who have not experienced this humanizing in relation to the world will lack something of humanity in later years. Teachers must be willing to enter the children's environment with their whole spirit and soul, so that children can go along with them on the strength of living experience.

All of this implies that much will have happened to our teachers before they enter the classroom. The accomplishment of these educational principles places great demands on the preparation that teachers must do. As much as possible must be done ahead of time if teachers are to make the best use of their time in the classroom. Teachers learn to do this only gradually and with time, but it is only through this slow and gradual learning that teachers acquire a true regard for the individuality of children.

May I speak of a personal experience in this connection? Years before my relationship with the Waldorf school, I had to deal with many forms of education. Thus it happened that when I was still young, I was charged with the education of a boy of eleven who was exceedingly backward in his development. Until then, he had learned nothing at all. As proof of his achievements, I was shown an exercise book containing the results of the latest examination he had been forced into. All that could be seen there was an enormous hole he had made with an eraser; nothing else. In addition to this, the boy's domestic habits were pathological. The whole family was unhappy because of him, since they could not bring themselves to abandon him to a manual occupation—a social prejudice, if you like, but we must deal with such prejudices. So the whole family was unhappy. The family doctor was explicit that nothing could be done with the boy.

So I was given all four children of this family to educate. The others were normal, and I was to educate this one along with them. I said that I would try; in such a case, one cannot make promises that something will be achieved. I decided to do everything within my power, but told them that I must have complete freedom in his education. His mother was the only member of the family who understood my stipulation for freedom, which meant that his education had to be fought for with the others. But ultimately, the boy's instruction was left to me.

It was necessary that the time spent in the boy's immediate instruction be as brief as possible. Thus, if I had to teach the boy for, say, about a half hour, I had to prepare for three hours so that I could use of the time most economically. Moreover, I had to carefully note the time of his music lesson, for example, because if the boy became overworked he turned pale and his health deteriorated. However, because I understood the boy's whole pathological condition, and because I understood the hydrocephalic condition, it was possible to make progress with the boy—and not just soul progress. Such was his progress that, just a year and a half after he had shown me merely a hole in his exercise book, he was able to enter high school. And I was able to help him further through his classes in high school and follow up with him until almost the end of his time there.

Under the influence of this education, and also because everything was spiritually directed, the boy's head became smaller. I know that a doctor might say that his head may have become smaller anyway. Certainly, but the right care of spirit and soul had to accompany that process. The person I've been speaking of later became an excellent doctor. He died during the war while performing his profession, though not until he was nearly forty years old.

It was especially important in this case to achieve the greatest economy of instruction time through the appropriate preparation. This must now become a general principle, and it is what we work for in the art of education I am talking about. When we teach by describing what we have to say to children in ways that arouse liveliness in their whole being, we must first master the subject thoroughly ahead of time, and we must be so at home with the material that we can direct all our attention and individual power to the form in which we present it. Then we discover naturally that all our teaching must become pictorial if children are to grasp it not just intellectually but with their whole being. So we usually begin with stories such as fairy tales or made-up stories related to nature. We do not begin by teaching language or any other subject; we simply unfold the world itself in vivid pictures before the children. Such instruction is the best preparation for writing and reading, which will be derived imaginatively.

Thus, between their ninth and tenth years, children come to express themselves in writing and have learned to read as far as it is healthy at this age. We have now reached that important point in a child's life, between the ninth and tenth years, which I have already mentioned. You must realize that this important point in a child's life also manifests externally. A very remarkable change takes place—the differentiation between girls and boys. I will speak later about the significance of this for a coeducational school such ours. In the meantime, we must bear in mind that the differentiation between boys and girls does take place. Thus, around the tenth year, girls begin to grow more quickly than do boys. Growth in boys is held back, and girls overtake them in growth. When children reach puberty, the boys again catch up with the girls and the boys begin to grow more quickly.

Between the tenth and fifteenth years, the outer differences between girls and boys indicate that a significant phase of life has been reached. Inwardly, a clear distinction between oneself and the world appears. Before this time, there was no such thing as a plant—only a green thing with red flowers in which there is a little spirit, just as there is a little spirit in us. With plants, such things do not make sense to children until around the tenth year. Here we must be able to follow their feeling. Thus, only when children reach this age is it correct to teach them about the external world of our surroundings.

One can begin, for example, with botany, a great stand-by for schools. But, particularly in the case of botany, I can show how one should conduct a formal education (in the best sense of the word). It is completely unnatural to begin by showing children a single plant, because it is not a whole. A plant is not whole, especially when it has been taken from the ground. In our age of realism and materialism, people have little sense for what is material and natural, otherwise they would have a feeling for what I have just said. Is a plant whole? No; once we pull it from the earth and bring it here, it quickly withers. It is not natural to be pulled up. Its nature is to be in the earth with the soil. A stone is complete in itself. It can lie anywhere, and it makes no difference. But I cannot carry a plant all over the place; it will change. Its nature is complete only in conjunction with the soil and the forces that spring from the earth, along with all the sun's forces that fall on this particular piece of earth. Together with these, the plant makes a totality. To view a plant in isolation is absurd; it's like pulling a hair out of one's head and regarding the hair itself as complete. A hair arises in connection with an organism and cannot be understood apart from that organism. Therefore, when teaching botany, we must not begin with the plant or plant family but with the landscape and geography. We must begin with an understanding of what the earth is like in a particular place. The nature of plants must be treated in relation to the whole earth.

When we speak of the earth, we generally speak as physicists or, at most, as geologists. We assume that the earth is a self-enclosed totality of physical, mineral forces, and that its existence would be no different if there were no plants, animals, or people at all. But this is an abstraction. The earth as viewed by the physicist or geologist is an abstraction. There is, in fact, no such thing. In reality there is simply the earth covered with plants. We must be aware that, when our description is purely geological, it is only for the convenience of our intellect, and that we are describing a non-existent abstraction. We must not start by giving children an idea of this non-existent abstraction; rather, we must give them a realization of the earth as a living organism, beginning, of course, with the area that the children know. If children know nothing of an animal, we would not show them just a hair; we would show them animal with hair growing on it. Similarly, we must begin by giving children a vivid realization of the earth as a living organism, and then show them how plants live and grow on the earth.

The introduction to the animal kingdom is entirely different and comes a little later. Again, to describe the single animals is inorganic. Indeed, it could almost be said that it is pure chance that a lion is a lion and a camel a camel. A lion presented to a child's contemplation will seem arbitrary, no matter how well it is described, or even if it is seen in a menagerie. It is the same with a camel. Observation alone makes no sense in the area of life. Thus, the study of plants follows naturally from introducing the earth to children as a living organism, beginning with a particular region. To consider one part of the earth at a time, however, is also an abstraction, since no region can exist apart from the other regions. We should be aware that this involves beginning with something incomplete. In any case, if we teach with images and appeal to the wholeness of children's imagination, they will be alive to what we tell them about plants. In this way, we gradually introduce children to the external world. They gain a sense of objectivity and begin to live into reality. We do this by introducing children in a natural way to the plant kingdom.

And how are we to regard animals? Anyone who can contemplate animals with imaginative vision instead of abstract intellect finds that each animal is a portion of the human being. In one animal, the leg development predominates—whereas they are at the service of the whole organism in human beings. In another animal, the sense organs or a particular sense organ is developed in an extreme way. One animal will be specially adapted for smell, another for seeing from high in the air. When we look at the whole animal kingdom, we find that the external, abstract divisions of the animal kingdom together make up the human being. All the animals taken together, synthetically, represent a single human being. Each capacity or group of faculties in the human being is expressed in a one-sided way in an animal species. When we study an animal, there is no need to explain everything to children; we can show them in simple pictures. When we study lions, for example, we find particularly overdeveloped heart and chest organs. Cows show a one-sided development of the digestive system. And when I examine the white corpuscles of human blood, I see an indication of the earliest, most primitive creatures. The whole animal kingdom together is a synthesis of the human being, not symptomatically, but synthetically woven and interwoven.

I can explain all of this to children in a simple, primitive way. Indeed I can make it very vivid when speaking, for instance, about the lion's nature and showing how it needs to be calmed and subdued by the human individuality. Or we can take the moral and soul characteristics of the camel, showing how the camel presents, in a lower form, what we find in human nature. The human being is a synthesis of lion, eagle, ape, camel, cow, and all the rest. We can view the whole animal kingdom as human nature divided up and spread out.

So this is the other side that children get during their eleventh or twelfth year. After they have learned to separate themselves from the plant world—to experience objectivity and a connection with an objective earth—they then learn of the close connection between animals and human beings—the subjective side. Thus the universe is again connected with the human being through feelings. In this way, we educate children through contact with life in the world.

Thus, we find that the requirements we establish are met spontaneously. In theory, we can keep saying that we must not overload the memory. It is not good to burden children's memory, and anyone can see that in the abstract. It is more difficult to see clearly how an overburdened memory affects a person's life. It means that later in life the person suffers from rheumatism and gout. It is a pity that medical observation does not cover the whole span of a life, but in fact we find many people who are afflicted with rheumatism and gout, to which they had no predisposition. Or perhaps a slight predisposition was increased because the memory was overtaxed, because one was forced to learn too much from memory. On the other hand, the memory must not be neglected, because if the memory is not exercised enough inflammatory conditions of the physical organs are likely to arise, particularly between sixteen and twenty-four.

So how can we maintain a balance between burdening the memory and neglecting it? When we teach with images and with imagination (as I have described), children take as much instruction as they can bear. A relationship arises like that between eating and being satisfied. This means that we will have some children who are more advanced than others, and we must deal with this without placing less advanced children in a lower class. You may have a relatively large class, and yet a child will not eat more than is bearable, spiritually, because the organism spontaneously rejects what a child cannot bear. Thus, here we consider life, just as we draw our teaching from life.

Children are able to take in the elements of arithmetic at a very early age. But in arithmetic we can see how easy it is to give an intellectual element to children too early. Mathematics per se is not alien to anyone at any age. It arises from human nature; the principles of mathematics are not foreign to human nature as letters are foreign in a succeeding civilization. It is exceedingly important, however, that children be introduced to arithmetic and mathematics in the right way. And this can really be determined only by those enabled to oversee the whole of human life from a certain spiritual standpoint.

Arithmetic and moral principles are two things that, in terms of logic, seem very removed from each other. It is not common to connect arithmetic with moral principles, because the logical connection is not obvious. It is obvious, however, to those who

The Art of Educating Older Boys and Girls   71

do not view the matter in terms of logic but in a living way that children who are introduced to arithmetic correctly will have a very different feeling of moral responsibility than those who were not. Now, what I am about to say may seem like an extreme paradox to you, but since I am speaking of realities and not of the illusions of our age, I will not fear the seemingly paradoxical, for these days truth often seems paradoxical. If people had known how to permeate the soul with mathematics in the right way during these past years, we would not now have Bolshevism in Eastern Europe. One perceives the forces that connect the faculty used in arithmetic with the springs of morality in humankind.

Perhaps you will understand this better if I give you a little illustration of the principles behind teaching arithmetic. Today it is common to begin arithmetic by adding one thing to another. But just consider how alien it is to the human mind when we add one pea to another, and with each addition specify a new name. The transition from one to two and then to three; such counting is an arbitrary activity for the human being. It is possible, however, to count in a different way. We find this when we go back a little in human history. Originally, people did not count by adding one pea to another and deriving a new thing that, for the soul anyway, had little to do with what came before. Rather, people counted more or less as follows. It was their view that everything in life can always be grasped as a whole, and the most diverse things might constitute a unity. If I have a number of people in front of me, that can be a unity at first. Or if I have an individual before me, that person is a unity. A unity, in reality, is purely relative.

Now, I keep this in mind as I count in this way:

|—————1—————| |——1——|——2——| |——1——|——2——|——3——|

In other words, I take an organic whole—a whole consisting of members. I begin with unity, and in that unity, viewed as a multiplicity, I seek the parts. This, in fact, was the original view of number. Unity was always a totality, and one looked for the parts in the whole. One did not think of numbers as arising from the addition of one and one and one; rather, one conceived of the numbers as belonging to a whole and proceeding organically from that whole.

When we apply this to teaching arithmetic, we get the following: instead of placing one bean after another for children to see, we give them a whole pile of beans. The bean pile constitutes a whole, and we begin with this. Next, with our pile of beans (or a pile of apples if you think it might appeal more to their imagination), we explain that there are three children of various ages who need different amounts to eat. We want to do something that might apply to real life. So, what shall we do? We could, for example, divide the pile of apples so that we have one pile, on the one hand, and, on the other, two portions that together equal to the first pile. The whole pile represents the sum. We have a pile of apples, and we say, "Here are three parts." And we get the children to see that the sum equals the three parts. In other words, in addition we do not go from the parts and arrive at the sum; we begin with the sum and proceed to the parts. Thus, to get a living understanding of addition, we begin with the whole and proceed to the addenda, or parts. Addition is concerned essentially with the sum and its parts—the members contained, one way or another, in the sum.

This is how we get children to enter life with the ability to grasp the whole, rather than always proceeding from less to more. This has a very powerful influence on a child's whole soul and mind. Once children have acquired the habit of adding things together, a disposition arises that tends to be desirous and craving. By proceeding from the whole to the parts, on the other hand, and by treating multiplication in a similar way, children are less prone to acquisitiveness. Instead, they tend to develop, in the noblest Platonic sense, consideration and moderation. Our moral likes and dislikes are intimately connected with the way we learned to deal with numbers. At first sight, it's difficult to see any logical connection between one's approach to numbers and moral ideas. Indeed, those who look at things only from the intellectual point of view may laugh at the idea of a connection; it may seem absurd to them. It is also easy to understand that people may laugh at the idea of going from the sum in addition, instead of from the parts. When one sees the true connections in life, however, the things that seem most remote logically become exceedingly close.

Consequently, the processes that take place in the souls of children through working with numbers have a tremendous effect on the way they meet us when we wish to present them with moral examples and actions intended to evoke sympathy for good and antipathy toward evil. We will see children who are open to goodness if we have taught them numbers as described.

Teachers As Artists in Education

August 22, 1922

It is important for educators to understand the whole human being, and this becomes an imperative when we begin to observe the development of boys and girls between the eleventh and twelfth years. One ususally fails to observe the more subtle changes and sees only the obvious transformations of human nature. Consequently, we believe we can help children merely by deciding which bodily movements should become physically stronger. However, to make their bodies strong, capable, and free of restrictions, we must reach the body during childhood through soul and spirit.

Between the eleventh and twelfth years, a great change takes place in the human being. The rhythmic system—breathing and blood circulation—dominates between the change of teeth and puberty. When children are almost ten years old, the rhythms of the blood and breathing systems begin to develop and flow more into the muscular system. The muscles become saturated with blood, and the blood pulses through the muscles in intimate response to inner human nature and the heart. Thus, between ten and twelve people build up the rhythmic system in a way that corresponds to their inner disposition. When children reach eleven or twelve, what lives in the rhythmic system and muscular system is passed into the skeletal system. Until the eleventh year, the skeletal system is wholly embedded in and conforms to the muscular system. Between eleven and twelve, the skeleton adapts to the external world. A mechanic and dynamic quality that is independent of the human being passes into the skeleton. We must become accustomed to seeing the skeleton as if it were an entirely objective thing and not concerned with the human being.

When observing children younger than eleven, we see that all their movements still come from their inner being. When we observe the way children over twelve walk, we see how they are trying to find their balance, inwardly adapting to leverage and balance and the mechanical nature of the skeletal system. This means that, between eleven and twelve, the nature of soul and spirit reaches all the way into the skeleton. Before this time, the nature of soul and spirit is much more inward. At this point, one has taken hold of the most remote aspect of human nature, the skeleton, and one's adaptation to the outer world is complete. Only now do we become a true child of the world; we live now with the mechanistic dynamic of the world, and now does we experience so-called causality in life. Before the eleventh year, people really have no understanding of cause and effect. We hear the words and think we understand them, but we do not, because we control the skeletal system through the muscular system. Later, after the twelfth year, as the skeleton adjusts to the outer world, it dominates the muscular system and influences spirit and soul through it. As a result, one now begins to understand cause and effect based on inner experience, an understanding of force. We begin to understand our experience of vertical and horizontal and so on.

Because of all this, we harm their development if we teach children mineralogy, physics, chemistry, or mechanics in a way that is too intellectual for children before the eleventh year, because they do not yet have a corresponding experience of their inner mechanical and dynamic nature. Nor can children inwardly participate in the causal relationships in history before their eleventh year.

This tells us how to treat the souls of children before the skeletal system has awakened. Children can inwardly experience biography while they still live in the muscular system, through the intermediary of the blood system. They can always participate if we present specific historical images that please or displease them—images toward which they can feel sympathy or antipathy. Or we can present images of the earth, as I described yesterday. They can take in images related to the plant kingdom, because the muscular system is inwardly pliable. We can also show them what I explained about animals and how that whole kingdom exists in a human being; a child can go along with this, because the muscular system is soft.

On the other hand, if we teach children about the principle of levers or the steam engine before they reach eleven, they cannot experience this inwardly, because the dynamic of their own physical nature has not yet developed. If we begin physics, mechanics, and dynamics at the right time (when children are about eleven or twelve), whatever we present in thinking goes into the head and is met by what comes from their inner being—the experience of their own skeletal system. What we say to them unites with the impulse and experience that arises from the body. Thus a soul understanding arises instead of an abstract, intellectual understanding. This must be our goal.

But what about teachers who must accomplish this? What should they be like? Imagine a teacher, for example, who knows from anatomy and physiology where all the muscle and bones are and what nerve cells look like. This is all very well, but it is intellectual knowledge and does not take the children into account; they become, as it were, impermeable to one's vision. The children are opaque as black coal. One may know all the muscles and nerves but not how the circulatory system plays into the skeletal system. If we are to understand this, our concept of the human makeup and inner configuration must be that of an artist. Teachers must be in a position to experience children as artists would. They must see everything in children as inwardly pliable.

Now, a philosopher might say, "Well, if something is to be known it must be logical." This is true, but this must be the logic of a work of art, which may be an inner representation of the world we see. We must accept an inner artistic idea and not dogmatically believe that the world has to be conceived logically. The ideas and feelings of teachers must be flexible. Teachers must realize that, if they present ideas of dynamics and mechanics to children before they reach eleven, they congest the brain and make it inflexible, so that as they grow it develops migraine and, later still, hardens. On the other hand, if we give children isolated historical images or stories before the eleventh year; if we present pictures of the plant kingdom that show plants in connection with the countryside where they grow, such ideas go into the brain, but they go there by way of the rest of the nervous system into the whole body. They unite with the soft muscular system and the whole body. We lovingly build what is working within the children.

Thus, teachers see into children. Those who know only anatomy and physiology see children as opaque coal, but here they become transparent and teachers see everything. They see what goes on in the individual children at their desks. Teachers do not need to cogitate and resort to some didactic rule; the children themselves show them what needs to be done. Children lean back in their chairs and no longer pay attention when something is done that is unsuitable for them. When you do the right thing for children, they become lively.

Of course, we will occasionally have a lot of trouble trying to control this liveliness in children. You can control it, however, if you have something that is not appreciated enough in such cases: a sense of humor. Teachers must bring humor when they enter the classroom. Sometimes children can be very mischievous. There was one Waldorf teacher whose class of children over twelve suddenly became inattentive to the lesson and began passing notes to one another under their desks. Of course, a teacher without a sense of humor might become angry, and there would be a big scene. But she went right along with them and explained how the postal service works, and the children realized that she understood them. Shee went directly into the matter of mutual correspondence. They felt a bit ashamed and order was restored.

The fact is, no art can be mastered without humor, especially the art of dealing with human beings. This means that the art of education involves eliminating ill humor and anger from teachers. It means developing friendliness and love full of humor and fantasy for the children; otherwise, the children see in their teacher the very thing they are forbidden to be. A class teacher must never respond to a child's anger by threatening to beat the anger out of that child. That would be terrible. Or a teacher might respond by grabbing something and throwing it to the ground where it is smashed. This is not a way to remove anger from a child. The proper way to act as an educator is to show children that anger is a mere object, and that for you it barely exists and should be treated with humor.

Until now I have been describing how the human being should be understood in general by teachers. But people are not just something "in general." Even if we study the human being in such detail that we see clearly into the very activity of the muscular system before the eleventh year and into the skeletal system after the eleventh year, something extraordinarily vital still remains to be understood for the art of education: human individuality. Each child is different, and what I have described thus far is only the very first step in an artistic understanding of children. We must enter more and more into what is personal and individual. Provisionally, we are helped by the fact that the children we educate have different temperaments. From the very beginning, a real understanding of temperaments has been very important for the education I am describing as practiced in a Waldorf school.

Let us begin by looking at melancholic children, a particular human type. What are they like? Externally, they seem quiet and withdrawn, but these outer characteristics do not help us much. We begin to comprehend children with a melancholic disposition only when we realize that they are affected most powerfully by their purely physical nature, and when we understand that melancholia is the result of an intense deposit of salt in the organism. This causes melancholic children to feel weighed down in the physical organism. It is a very different experience for a melancholic child to raise an arm or leg than it is for other children; there are impediments to raising an arm or leg. A feeling of weight opposes the soul's intention. Consequently, melancholic children gradually turn inward and do not enter the outer world with any pleasure, because the body is of such concern and intrudes on their attention. We can approach melancholic children correctly only when we realize how their soul and spirit would soar if they were not burdened by the bodily deposits continuously secreted by glands, which permeate other bodily movements and encumber the body. We can help them only when we correctly understand this encroaching physical heaviness that imprisons their attention.

It is often said that melancholic children brood inwardly, and that they are quiet and move very little. As a result, one purposely urges them to take in lively ideas, trying to heal through the opposite. One's treatment of melancholics is to enliven them by saying all sorts of amusing things. But this method is completely wrong. We cannot reach melancholic children this way. Through sympathy and understanding of their physical gravity, we must approach children in their own individual mood. Thus we do not give melancholics lively and comical ideas, but serious ideas like those they produce themselves. Whatever we give them must be in harmony with the tone of their own burdened organism.

Further, in education such as this, we must be patient; the effect is not immediate but takes years. It works like this: when children receive from outside what they have within themselves, it arouses within them the healing forces of resistance. If we bring them something foreign, such as something comic to a serious child, they remain indifferent. But if we confront them externally with their own sorrow and woe, they perceive what they have in themselves, and this evokes the opposite inner response. Thus, we heal pedagogically by adapting the ancient golden rule to a modern method: Like not only recognizes like; like can heal like.

When we consider children of a more phlegmatic temperament, we must realize that they live less in the physical body and more in what I call the ether body; this is a more volatile body. It may seem odd to say that phlegmatic children live in their ether body, but this is how it is. The ether body prevents the human processes of digestion and growth from entering the head. It is not in the power of phlegmatic children to conceive of what is going on in the body; the head becomes inactive. The body becomes increasingly active because of the volatile element that tends to scatter their activities into the world. Phlegmatic children are entirely surrendered to and absorbed into the world. They live very little within themselves, so they respond with a certain indifference toward what we to do with them. We cannot reach them, because immediate access must go through the senses. The principle senses are in the head, but phlegmatic children make little use of the head. The rest of the organism functions through interplay with the outer world.

Again, as with melancholic children, we can reach phlegmatic children only when, as artists, we can turn ourselves into phlegmatics of some sort. Then they have at their side what they are in themselves, and with time this will seem too boring. Even phlegmatics eventually find a phlegmatic teacher boring. And, if we are patient, we will see how something lights up in phlegmatic children if we present ideas calmly and speak to them phlegmatically about uninteresting events.

Sanguine children are especially difficult. The activity of the rhythmic system very much dominates in them. The rhythmic system, which is dominant between the change of teeth and puberty, dominates sanguine children too much. Sanguine children, therefore, always want to move rapidly from one impression to another, and their blood circulation becomes hampered if impressions do not change quickly enough. They feel inwardly restricted if impressions do not pass quickly and give way to others. So we can say that sanguine children feel an inner constriction if they have to stay with any one thing too long, and they turn away to very different thoughts. It is hard to hold them.

Once more, the treatment of sanguine children is similar to that of the others; we must not try to balance sanguine children by forcing them to stay for a longer period with one impression, but do the opposite. Meet the sanguine nature by changing impressions vigorously, making sure they have to take in impression after impression in rapid succession. Again, a response will be called into play, and this will certainly take the form of antipathy toward the fast pace of impressions, because the circulatory system dominates entirely. The result will be that the sanguine child slows down.

Choleric children must be treated in yet another way. Choleric children are typically a step behind normal in development. This may seem strange, but let us take an illustration. Any normal children of eight or nine move their limbs quickly or slowly in response to outer impressions. But compare eight- or nine-year-old children with those of three or four, who still trip and dance through life and have far less control of their movements. They still retain something of the baby in them. Babies do not control their movements at all, but kick around because the mental forces are not yet developed. But if tiny babies had a vigorous mental development, you would find them to be cholerics. Kicking babies—and the healthier they are, the more they kick—are all choleric. Choleric children come from a body made restless by choler. Cholerics retain something of the romping and raging of a tiny baby. Thus, the baby lives on in choleric boys and girls of eight or nine. This is why a child is choleric, and we must treat the child by trying gradually to subdue the baby within.

In doing this, humor is essential. When we confront a true choleric of eight to ten or even older, we will accomplish nothing through admonition. But if I get this child to recount a story I have told previously—a story that requires a display of great choler and much pantomime—the child will sense the baby within, and this will have the effect gradually calming the "tiny baby." Children will adapt it to the stage of their own mind. When I act choleric toward a choleric child—naturally, with humor and complete self-control—the child will grow calmer. When teachers begin to dance (please do not misunderstand me), the raging child nearby gradually subsides. But one must avoid having a red or sad face when dealing with choleric children; one must enter this inner rage by means of an artistic sensibility. You will see that the child will become more and more quiet. This completely subdues the inner raging.

This must not, however, be the least bit artificial. If there is anything forced or inartistic in what the teacher does, it will have no result. Teachers must indeed have artist's blood in them, so that what they enact in front of the children will seem real and be accepted without question; otherwise, it will be something false in the teacher, and that must be avoided. A teacher's relationship to the child must be absolutely genuine.

When we approach the temperaments in this way, it also helps us to keep even a very large class in order. Waldorf teachers study the temperaments of those children entrusted to them. They know that they have children who are melancholic, phlegmatic, sanguine, and choleric. They place the melancholics together, unobtrusively and without it being noticed, of course. They know they have these children in this corner. The one places the cholerics together and knows they are in another corner, and so on with the sanguines and phlegmatics. Using this social treatment, those of like temperament rub one another's corners off, so to speak. For example, a melancholic becomes cheerful when sitting among other melancholics. As for the cholerics, they heal each other thoroughly, since it is best to let cholerics work off their choler on one another. If bruises are exchanged, it has a very sobering effect. Through the right social treatment the underlying interrelationships can be brought into a healthy resolution.

The point is this: by way of the temperaments, one gets closer and closer to the individuality of the children and their personalities. Today, many people say that you must educate individually. This is true, but you must first discover the individual. First you must know the human being, then you must know the melancholic. In reality, a melancholic child is never purely melancholic; the temperaments are always mixed. One temperament dominates, and once you understand the temperament correctly, you can find your way to the individual. And if we have a good enough sense of humor, we may send a boy who is overwrought by rage into the garden, and watch him climb trees and scramble around until he is truly tired out. And when he returns, he will have worked off his choleric temper on himself and with nature. Once he has worked off what is in him by overcoming obstacles, he will return after awhile calmed down.

This indeed shows that the art of education must be learned intimately. People today do not judge clocks, or at least I have not heard it. People do not usually consider the merits of a clockwork, because they do not understand how it functions. Thus you seldom hear a clockwork judged in ordinary conversation. But you hear people judging education wherever you go. Often it sounds as though people are talking about the works of a clock, about which they haven't the slightest knowledge. People do not realize that education must be intimately learned and that it is not good enough to state abstractly that we must "educate the individual." First we must discover the individuality by gaining an intimate knowledge of the human being and the various temperaments. Then we gradually approach what is uniquely individual in a person. This must become a life principle, particularly for artistic teachers.

Everything depends on the contact between teachers and children, which must be permeated by an artistic element. This will bring about—intuitively, almost instinctively—much that teachers must do whenever an individual child comes to them. Let us use a concrete illustration for the sake of clarity. Suppose we find it difficult to educate a certain boy, because all the images we bring him—the impressions we wish to arouse, the ideas we would give—set up such a strong circulation in his head and disturb his nervous system so much that whatever we give cannot escape the head and go into the rest of his organism. The physical organism of the head becomes somewhat melancholic, in a sense. The boy finds it difficult to take what he experiences from his head into the rest of his organism. What he learns gets stuck, as it were, in the head. It cannot penetrate down into the rest of the organism. Artists in education will instinctively keep such a thing in mind in any specifically artistic work with this child. If I have such a child, I will use colors and paint with him in a very different way than with other children. Because it is so important, from the very beginning we give special attention to color in the Waldorf school. I have already explained the principle of the painting, but in the painting lesson we can treat each child individually. We have an opportunity to work individually with children, because they must do everything themselves.

Now suppose I have a child such as I described. I am taking the painting lesson. If the right artistic contact exists between teacher and child, under my guidance this child will produce a very different painting from other children.

I will draw roughly on the blackboard what would appear on a paper painted by the child whose ideas are stuck in the head. Something of this sort should arise: Here a spot of yellow, then further on a spot of, say, orange, for we have to keep in mind the harmony of colors. Next comes a transition to violet, and the transition may be differentiated more, and then to make an outer boundary, the whole may be enclosed in blue. This is what we get on the paper of a child whose ideas are congested in his head.

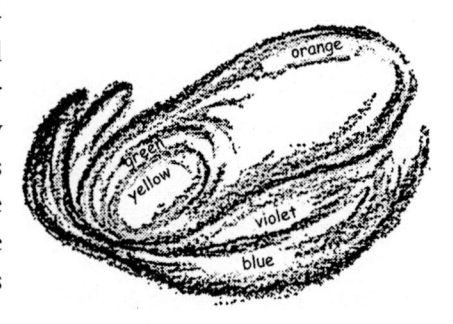

Now suppose I have another child whose ideas, far from sticking in his head, sift through the head as through it were a sieve; everything goes into the body, and the child grasps nothing because the head is like a sieve with holes, allowing things to go through as it sifts everything. We must be able to sense that in this child the circulatory system of the other part of the organism wants to draw everything into itself.

Then one intuitively decides to get the child to do something different. In the case of this child, you will get something like this on paper. Observe how much less the colors go into curves, or rounded forms; rather, you find the colors drawn out, the painting approximates drawing, and we get loops that are more proper to drawing. You will also notice that the colors are not differentiated much; in the first drawing, they are strongly differentiated and here there is not much differentiation.

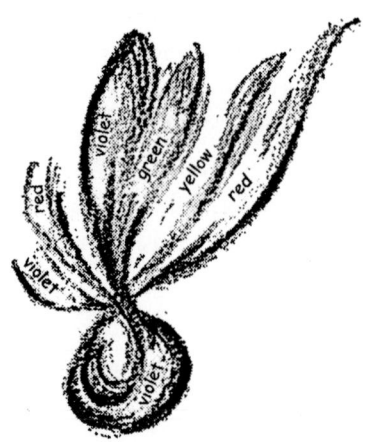

If one does this with real colors (not with the nauseating substance of chalk, which does not give an idea of the whole), then through the experience of pure color in the one case, and more formed color in the other, we can work back upon the characteristics of the child I described.

Similarly, when you go into the gym with a boy or girl whose ideas stick in the head, your goal will be different than if you were there with a child whose head is like a sieve, allowing everything through into the circulation of the rest of the body. You take both kinds of children into the gym with you. You get the one group, whose heads are like a sieve, to alternate gymnastic exercises with recitation or singing. The other gymnastic group, whose ideas are stuck in their heads, should do their movements as much as possible in silence. In this way, you create a bridge between physical training and soul characteristics, out of the very nature of children themselves. Children who have stuck ideas must do gymnastics differently from those whose ideas simply flow through the head.

This sort of thing shows how very important it is to compose education as a whole. It is terrible when a teacher first instructs children in a classroom, and then they are sent off to the gym, while the gymnastic teacher knows nothing of what has happened in class and simply follows a separate scheme in the gymnastic lesson. The gymnastic lesson must follow absolutely from what was experienced with children in class. In practice, therefore, the Waldorf school tries as much as possible to trust to one teacher even supplementary lessons in the lower classes, and certainly all that concerns general human development.

This makes tremendous demands on the staff, especially in teaching art. It also demands the most willing and loving devotion. But there is no other way we can we attain a wholesome, healing human development.

Now, in the lectures that follow, I will describe on the one hand certain modeled and painted figures made in the studio at Dornach, so we can acquaint you better with eurythmy, the art of movement that is so intimately related to the whole human being. The figures bring out the colors and forms of eurythmy and something of its inner quality. On the other hand, I will speak tomorrow about painting and other artistic work by the younger and older children in the Waldorf school.

The Organization of the Waldorf School

August 23, 1922

When we speak of organization today, we generally refer to something structured or prearranged. But when speaking of the Waldorf school organization, I do not mean it in this sense, for really we cannot organize something unless it has a mechanistic nature. One can organize the arrangement of a factory, using ideas to assemble into a whole what one has put into it. The whole exists, and one must accept it as an organism. It must be studied. One must learn how it is arranged as an organization.

The Waldorf school is an organism in this sense, of course, but it cannot be organized in the sense of making a program to establish how the school will be run according to sections one, two, three, and so on. As I said, I am fully convinced that if five or a dozen people sit down together today (and I say this without irony), they can work out an ideal school plan that cannot be improved upon. People are so intelligent and smart today, establishing paragraphs one, two, up to twelve, and so on—the only question is, can it be put into practice? And it would soon become clear that, whereas people can create lovely programs, when it comes to establishing the school itself we must deal with a finished organism. Thus, this school is made up of a staff of teachers who are not molded out of wax. Section one or five might state that a teacher shall be such and such. But the staff is not made up of something we can shape like wax; we have to seek out each teacher and then accept the faculties that come with that individual.

Most important, it is necessary to understand what these faculties are. First we must know whether a person will make a good elementary teacher or might be better for the upper classes. It is important to understand the teachers as individuals, including their human organism—the nose or the ear—if we really want to accomplish something. It is not a matter of theoretical principles and rules but a matter of meeting reality as it comes. If teachers could be shaped from wax, we could make programs. But this cannot be done. So the first reality to deal with is the college of teachers, and we must know this intimately. Thus it is a fundamental principle of the organization of the Waldorf school that, because I am its director and spiritual adviser, I must know each individual of the college of teachers intimately.

Second is the children; here we were faced immediately with certain practical difficulties in the Waldorf school, for it was founded in Stuttgart by Emil Molt amid the emotions and impulses of 1918 and 1919, right after the war. It was initially established as a social action. One could see that not much could be done with adults in terms of society; they gained some understanding in Central Europe for a few weeks after the war. After that, they fell back on the views of their various classes. So the idea arose to do something for the next generation. And because Mr. Molt happened to be an industrialist in Stuttgart, we had no need to go from house to house canvassing for children; we received the children of the workers in his factory. Thus, at the beginning, the children we received from Mr. Molt's factory—about 150 of them—were essentially proletarian children. Added to these were almost all the children of anthroposophists in Stuttgart and the neighborhood. So we had about two hundred children to work with at the beginning.

This situation meant that the school was, for all practical purposes, a school for all classes. For we had a foundation of proletarian children, and the children of anthroposophists were mostly not proletarian, but included every status from the lowest to the highest. Consequently, any class distinctions were ruled out in the school because of its social composition. The goal throughout has been, and will continue to be, to consider only what is universally human. In the Waldorf school, we considered the educational principles, and we make no difference in applying them, whether we are dealing with a child of the proletariat or the child of a former kaiser (supposing one had sought to enter the school). Educational and didactic principles will be all that counts. Thus, from the very beginning, the Waldorf school was considered a general school.

But of course this involved certain difficulties, because the habits proletarian children bring into the school are different from those of children from other classes. These contrasts, in fact, turned out to be very beneficial, apart from a few small issues that were handled with little trouble. You can easily imagine what these matters were; they mostly concern habits of life, and often it is not easy to rid children of all they bring with them to the school. But even this is possible if it is done with good will. Nevertheless, many children of the so-called upper classes are unaccustomed to having this or that on them, and they would sometimes carry home something unpleasant, which led their parents to make some unpleasant comments.

As I said, here were the children—what I would call the smaller difficulties. A greater difficulty was the fact that the ideal of the Waldorf school is to educate strictly according to knowledge of the human being, giving children week after week whatever their nature requires.

To begin with, we set up the Waldorf school as an elementary school of eight classes, with children from around seven to about fifteen years old. They came at first from all sorts of different schools, and their levels of achievement varied widely—certainly not always what we would consider appropriate for a child of eight or eleven. So, during the first year we could not count on accomplishing our ideal in education. Nor could we simply proceed one, two, three, according to a plan, but had to proceed according to the individual children in each class.

Nevertheless, that would have been only a minor problem. The larger problem is this: no method of education, however ideal, should sever a person's connections in life. People are not abstract things to be put through an education and be finished with. A person is the child of particular parents and grows up as the product of a society. Once education is accomplished, a person must enter that society. You see, if you want to educate children of fourteen or fifteen according to a strict idea, they would probably meet the ideal, but they would lose their way and never find their place in modern life. Consequently, it has never been merely a matter of following an ideal in the Waldorf school. The point is to educate children so that they stay in touch with society as it exists today. There is no point in saying that society today is bad. Whether good or bad, we simply have to live in it. And this is the point: we have to live in it, and so we must not isolate the children from it. Thus I was confronted with the very difficult task of carrying out an educational ideal without losing contact with modern life.

Naturally, the educational authorities considered the methods of other schools as a kind of ideal. True, they always admitted that the ideal is not possible in practice and that we must simply do our best under the circumstances; life makes various demands. In practice, however, when we had to deal with them, they considered the existing arrangements set up by the state or other authorities to be the best. And they viewed an institution such as the Waldorf school as a kind of crank hobby or the whimsy of someone a little touched in the head.

You know, it's often possible to just let a crank school like this carry on and see what comes of it. In any case, it has to be dealt with. So I tried to come to terms with them through a compromise. In a memo, I asked them to allow us three years to try out my "whimsy," at the end of which our children would be advanced enough to enter conventional schools. So I worked out a memo. I showed them how, once the children had finished the third elementary class (in their ninth year), they would have reached a certain level and would be able to enter the fourth grade in another school. In the meantime, however, I said I wanted complete freedom to give the children, week by week, all that is needed according to a knowledge of the human being.

Then I requested freedom again from the ninth to twelfth years. At the end of the twelfth year, the children would have again reached a level that would enable them to enter an ordinary school. And the same thing was requested in relation to their graduation. It was similar with regard to the children (I mean, of course, the young ladies and gentlemen) who would be leaving school to enter college, university, or another school of higher education; from puberty until the time of entering college, there should be complete freedom. By that time, however, they should be advanced enough to enter any college or university, for it will, of course, be a long time before the free high school at Dornach will be approved for giving a qualification for going into life. This parallel arrangement with conventional schools was an attempt to harmonize our own intent and ideals with the existing situation. There is nothing impractical about our school; on the contrary, this "whimsy" aims in every way to have a practical application to life.

The Organization of the Waldorf School

There is no question of establishing the school along the lines of some bad invention; then it would indeed be a construction, not an organization. Rather, it is truly a matter of studying week by week the organization that exists. Then any observer of human nature (including the nature of children) will actually discover the most concrete pedagogical measures from month to month. A doctor, for example, does not state during the very first examination everything that must be done for a patient. A good doctor needs to keep a patient under observation, because the human being is an organism. This is even more true of an organism such as a school, which must become a continued study. After all, it is quite likely that, given the nature of our staff and children, say, in 1920, we will operate in a very different way than we might with our staff and children in 1924. Perhaps the staff will have increased and changed, and we will certainly have different children. Consequently, a neat set of a dozen or so rules would be useless. The experience gained day by day in the classroom is the only thing that matters.

The heart of the Waldorf school, in terms of organization, is the teachers' staff meeting. These meetings are held regularly, and when I can be in Stuttgart they are held under my guidance, but in other circumstances they are held at frequent intervals.[1] Here, before the assembled staff, all the teachers in the school discuss their classroom experiences in detail. These regular staff meetings have the effect of making the school into an organism, just as the human body is an organism by virtue of its heart. In these staff meetings, it is not the principles that are most important, but the willingness of teachers to live together in goodwill and the avoidance any form of competi-

---

1. For the full record of those meetings from 1919 to 1924, see *Faculty Meetings with Rudolf Steiner*, 2 vols. (Anthroposophic Press, 1998).

tion. It is most significant that if one teacher makes a suggestion to another, it helps only when it involves the love of each individual child. And by this I do not mean the kind of love that is usually spoken of, but the love of an artistic teacher.

This love has a different nuance than that of ordinary love. It is not like the sympathy we feel for a sick person, although this is a love of humanity. To treat a sick person (and please do not misunderstand me), we must also be able to love the illness. One must be able to speak of a "beautiful illness." Of course, for the patient it is very bad, but for the one who has to treat it, it is a beautiful illness. In certain circumstances, it can even be a magnificent illness. It may be very bad indeed for the patient, but for the those whose task it is to go into it and treat it lovingly, it can be a magnificent illness.

Similarly, there might be a boy who is a complete rascal because of his mischievous ways, but his ways are often extraordinarily interesting, and one can love him very much. For example, we have a very abnormal boy in the Waldorf school, a very interesting case. He has been at the school from the beginning and entered the first class. He would typically run straight at his teacher as soon as his back was turned and hit him. The teacher treated this rascal with extraordinary love and extraordinary interest. He would treat the boy with affection and lead him back to his place, showing no sign of having noticed he had been hit from behind. One can treat this child only by considering his whole background and environment. One must know the parental milieu in which he has grown up, and one must understand his pathology. Then, despite his mischievous ways, one can do something with him, especially if one can love this form of mischief. There is something lovable about a person who is exceptionally mischievous.

A teacher has to look at these things in a unique way. It is very important for teachers to develop this special love I am speaking of. Then, in the staff meeting, one can speak to the point. For nothing helps so much in dealing with normal children as having observed abnormal children. Healthy children are relatively difficult to study, because their every characteristic is toned down. We cannot easily observe a particular characteristic and how it relates to others. In abnormal children, where one complex predominates, we soon discover a way to treat a particular character complex, even if it involves a pathological treatment. And this experience can then be applied to normal children.

This, then, is the organization. Such as it is, it has brought credit to the Waldorf school insofar as the number of children has increased so rapidly. Whereas we began the school with about two hundred children, we now have nearly seven hundred. And they are from every class, so that the school is now organized as a general school in the best sense of the word. In most of the classes, particularly the lower, we have had to arrange parallel classes, because there are too many children for a single class. Thus we have first class A, first class B, and so on. This has, of course, placed increasingly great demands on the school. The whole organization is intended to be conceived out of what life presents, and every new child modifies its nature. With each new member, the organism requires a fresh approach and further study of the human being.

The schedule in the Waldorf school places the main lesson in the morning. In winter it begins at 8 or 8:15, in summer a little earlier. The special feature of the main lesson is that it eliminates the usual schedule. We have no schedule in the usual sense; instead, a single subject is taught throughout the first two-hour period in the morning, with a break for younger children. The subject is carried on for four to six weeks and taken to a certain level. After that, another subject takes its place. In the higher classes for children of eleven, twelve, and thirteen, instead of classes such as religion from eight to nine, natural history from nine to ten, arithmetic from ten to eleven—in other words, instead of being thrown from one thing to another—they have, say, four weeks of arithmetic in the morning during October, then three weeks of natural history, and so on. It may be argued that children might forget what they learn, because a comprehensive subject taken in this way is hard on the memory. This argument, however, must be answered through economy of instruction and the excellence of the teachers. The subjects are recapitulated only in the final weeks of the school year, when we gather, as it were, the year's work. In this way, children grow right into a subject.

The language lesson is, for us, a conversation lesson, and it is the exception to this arrangement. We begin teaching languages, as far as possible—English and French—in the youngest classes of the school, and children learn to speak these languages from the very beginning. As much as possible, the children also learn the language without the meaning being translated into their own language. Thus, the word in the foreign language is connected with the object, not with the word in German. In this way, children learn "table" afresh in a foreign language; they do not learn the foreign word as a translation of *Tisch*. Thus, they learn to enter right into a language other than their mother tongue, and this becomes especially evident with the younger children. Further, it is our practice to avoid giving the younger children any abstract, theoretical grammar. Children do not understand grammar until they are nine or ten, when they reach an important turning point. I will speak about this change when I deal with the boys and girls of the Waldorf school.

Language teaching is usually between ten and twelve in the morning. This is the time used to teach what lies outside the main lesson in the first part of the morning. Thus any form of religious instruction also takes place at this time. I will talk more about teaching religion, as well as about moral teaching and discipline, when I deal with the theme of boys and girls in the Waldorf school. For the moment, I wish to emphasize that afternoons are used for singing, music, and eurythmy lessons. We do this so that children may participate, as much as possible, with their whole being in their education.

Teaching and education as a whole appeal all the more to the children's whole being, because it is conceived as a whole in the heart of the teachers' meetings I described. This is especially noticeable when education moves from the domain of soul into the physical world and practical life. The school pays particular attention to this transition into physical and practical life. Thus we try to make sure the children learn to use their hands more and more. We begin with the way little children handle their toys and games, and we develop this into the more artistic crafts, but still in a way that comes naturally from the children.

This is the sort of thing we produce. [Rudolf Steiner shows the audience various toys.] This is typical of the sixth school year. Many of these things belong more to junior classes, but as I said, we have to make compromises and will be able to reach our ideal only later on. Then, what a child of eleven or twelve can do today, a child of nine will be able to do. The nature of the practical work is both spontaneous and artistic. The children work with their will on something they choose, not something already set. This leads to handwork or woodwork classes, where children carve and make all sorts of objects that they plan themselves.

One discovers how much children can bring forth when their education is based on real life. I will give you an example. We get the children to carve things that will be both artistic and useful. One can put things in this one, for example.

[Steiner holds up a sample.] We get the children to carve forms like this so that they get a feeling for form as it comes from themselves. The children thus make a form derived from their own volition and enjoyment. And this brings out something very remarkable. Suppose we have had a human anatomy class at some time with this group—something particularly important for the sixth class. We explained the shapes of the bones and skeletal system, as well as the outer form of the body and the functions of the human organism. Because the instruction has been given in an artistic form, as I described, the children have been alive to it and have really taken it in. It has reached into their volition and not remained just thoughts in their heads. When they begin to do things like this [a carved bowl], we see that it lives on in their hands. The forms will vary according to what we have been teaching; it comes out in these forms. From the children's sculpting work, we can tell what was done in the morning from eight to ten, because the instruction permeates the whole being.

This is achieved only by truly seeing the way things occur in nature. May I say something very heretical? People are very fond of giving dolls to children, especially pretty dolls. They fail to see that children really don't want this. They wave it away, but it is forced on them—pretty dolls, all painted. It is far better to give children a handkerchief, or, if you can't spare that, a piece of cloth. You tie it together, make the head here, paint the nose, two eyes, and so on. [Steiner demonstrates with his own handkerchief.] Healthy children much prefer to play with these than with the pretty dolls, because something is left to the imagination. The most magnificent doll with red cheeks and such leaves nothing for the imagination to do. The fine doll brings an inner emptiness to a child.

Now, how do we draw out of children the things they make? When the children in our sixth class begin to produce things out of their own feeling for form, they look like this, as you can see from this small example [a wooden doll] we brought with us. These things are just as they grow from the unique imagination of any child.

It is very important, however, to get children to see as early as possible that they wish to think of life as naturally flexible, not innately rigid. Thus, when we get children to create toys (which for them are serious things), we must make sure that the things have mobility. Children do something like this entirely on their own—to my mind a most remarkable fellow [a carved bear]. They also attach these strings without any outside suggestion, so that this little fellow can wag his tongue when the string is pulled like this. Children bring their own imagination into play; they make a cat, not just a nice cat, but just as it strikes them. It might be humped, without further ado, and very well done.

I consider it especially valuable for children to be involved, even in their toys, with things that move—not just static things, but things that can be manipulated. Thus, they make things that give them enormous joy in the process. They not only make realistic things, but invent little people like these gnomes and the like [Steiner displays more toys].

And children discover how to make more complicated toys such as this [temperament bird]; they are not told this can be made but are encouraged until they make such a lively toy on their own. You can see it looks very depressed and sad. [The head and tail of the toy can be moved up and down. They were up at first, and then Steiner moved them down.]

When children make something like this [yellow owl with movable wings], they get a wonderful satisfaction. This can be done by children of ten to fourteen. So far only the older children have done this, but eventually we intend to introduce it to the younger classes, and of course the forms will become simpler.

In addition to our handicraft teaching, there are other handwork lessons. Keep in mind that the boys and girls are always taught together in the Waldorf school, right up to the highest class. So, with some exceptions, of course, the boys learn to do the same things the girls do—although as we build the higher classes, there will have to be some differentiation. It is remarkable how readily the little boys knit and crochet, while the girls willingly do work usually given just to boys. This has a social effect as well—mutual understanding between the sexes, which is tremendously important today. We still tend to be very unsocial and prejudiced in this matter, so it is very good when we get the results I will describe now.

In Dornach, we had a small school like this. In the name of Swiss freedom, it is forbidden, and the best we can do is teach the more advanced young ladies and gentlemen, because Swiss freedom prohibits the existence of free schools that compete with state-run schools. Of course, such things are not merely a matter of education. Nevertheless, for awhile in Dornach we tried to run a small school of this nature, in which boys and girls worked together. This is a boys' work; it was done in Dornach by a little American boy of about nine [a tea cozy]. This is the work of a boy not a girl. And in a Waldorf school, as I have said, boys and girls work side by side in the handwork lessons. All kinds of things are made in handwork—and they work very well together. In these two pieces of work, for example [two small cloths], unless you look at the detail you cannot tell whether they were done by a boy or girl.

The upper classes currently include boys and girls of sixteen and seventeen. In these we teach spinning and weaving as an introduction to practical life, so that they make a connection with real life. And in this one area, we find a striking difference; boys do not want to spin like the girls, but choose to help them. The girls spin, and the boys wish to assist like attendant knights. So far, this is the only difference we have found; in the spinning lesson, the boys want to serve the girls. Apart from this, we have found that the boys do every kind of handwork.

You can see that the goal is to build up the handwork and needlework lesson in connection with what is learned in the painting lesson. And in the painting lesson, children are not taught to draw or make patterns. They learn to work freely and spontaneously with color itself. Therefore, it is very important that children have the right experience of color. The children learn nothing if you allow them to dip their brushes in the little blocks of color in an ordinary paint kit or use a palette when they paint. Children need to learn how to live with color. They should not paint from a palette or blocks of color but from a jar or mug containing the color dissolved in water. Then they get a feeling of how one color goes with another and feel the harmony of colors through inner experience.

This can prove difficult and inconvenient, and sometimes the classroom does not look its best after a painting lesson, since some children are clumsy and others are not well versed in matters of tidiness. Although this method can be problematic, enormous progress is possible when children find a direct connection with color in this way. They learn to paint from the living nature of color itself rather than trying to copy something in a naturalistic way.

Color and form thus seem to appear on their own on the paper. To begin with, both at the Waldorf school [in Stuttgart] and in Dornach, the children express their own experience of color when painting by placing one color beside another or by enclosing one color within others. Children go right into color, and, on their own, gradually produce form from color. As you see here, the form arises without any drawing involved, from color [Steiner shows one of the paintings by the Dornach children]. This is done by the somewhat more advanced children in Dornach, but the little children are taught the same principle in the Waldorf school. Here, for example, we have paintings that represent the painting taught in the Waldorf school; they show attempts to express the experience of color. This is not an attempt to paint an object, but to paint an experience of color. Representational painting comes much later. If they paint objects too early, something of their sense of living reality is lost and replaced by a sense for what is dead.

By working like this, when approaching a particular object, it becomes far livelier than it would without this foundation. Children who have already learned to live in color can, for example, make the island of Sicily look like this, and we get a map. Thus, artistic work can be related to teaching geography. Once children have acquired a sense of color harmony in this way, they begin to make various useful objects. They are not drawn first, but the children have acquired a feeling for color, so they will be able to paint or form something like this book cover. The important thing is to arouse in children a real feeling for life, and color and form have the power to lead right into life.

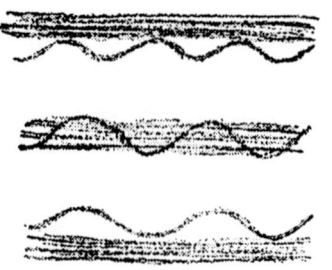

Now sometimes you'll see something terrible, such as when

The Organization of the Waldorf School

a teacher lets a child decorate a neck band, a waist band, and a dress hem, all of which use the very same pattern. One sees this occasionally. Naturally, to an artistic instinct it is the most horrible thing in the world. Child must be taught very early that a band designed for the neck has a tendency to open in a downward direction; that a waistband tends both up and down; and that the hem must show an upward direction, away from the bottom. We must not perpetrate the atrocity of teaching children to make a single artistic pattern, regardless of where it will appear on a person.

In the same way, one should be aware when making a book cover that, when a person looks at a book and opens it, there is a difference between top and bottom. Children need to grow into this feeling for space and form; it should penetrate right into their limbs. This way of teaching works far more strongly into the physical organism than any abstract work. Thus, the approach to color leads to making all sorts of useful objects; and in making these, children really come to feel the way colors work together, how forms affect one another, and that the whole has a purpose, and, therefore, one makes it just so. These details are essential to the vitality of the work; the lesson must be a preparation for life.

Among these exhibits you will find all sorts of interesting things; for example, this one is by a rather young girl. I cannot show everything during this lecture, but I would like to point to the many charming objects we brought from the Waldorf school. You will find two songbooks composed by Mr. Baumann that will show you the sort of songs and music we use. There are also various things produced by one of the girls. Because of the customs inspection, we could not bring a great deal with us besides ourselves. But all these things were formed, as you see here. The children have charming ideas [showing modeled monkeys]; they capture the life in nature.

And these are all carved in wood [showing illustrations of wood carvings].

With these [maps], you can see how fully children go into life when the principle they begin with is so full of life. You see this very clearly in these maps. First they have an experience of color, and this is a soul experience; color experience gives them a soul experience. Here you see Greece experienced in soul. When children are comfortable with color, they begin to sense that in geography they should paint the island of Crete in a certain color, the coast of Anatolia in another, and so on. Children learn to speak through color, and so a map can be produced from the innermost depths of the soul.

Think about the children's experience of the earth when they see it inwardly this way—when they paint Crete or Northern Greece this way and when their feelings correspond with colors such as these. Greece comes alive in the soul of a child; Greece can awaken in a new way from a child's soul. This is how the living reality of the world can become part of a human being. And when you confront these children later with the dry reality of everyday life, they respond in a very different way, because they have had an artistic, living experience of color in their simple paintings; they have learned to use its language.

Moral Teaching & Eurythmy in the Waldorf School

August 24, 1922

From what I have said already, you may now understand the goal of Waldorf education. It intends to bring up children to become strong and sound in body, free in soul, and clear in spirit. If children are to live in future society, it is most important that they have strong, healthy bodies, free souls, and clear spirits. And to educate in this way, teachers must have a thorough mastery of the principles I have tried to describe. Teachers must have a complete vision of the child's makeup—one that enables them to assess physical health. Only those who can truly judge physical health and harmonize it with the soul can understand the needs of each child as an individual.

It is accepted today that a doctor should have access to schools, and the system of school doctors is growing. However, we do not give the responsibility of teaching different subjects to various teachers who have no contact with one another, and neither should we give the responsibility of physical health to someone who is not a member of the staff or a member of the college of teachers. Such a situation presents a particular difficulty, which the following incident illustrates.

Once, when we were showing visitors through the Waldorf school, there was one gentleman whose official capacity was inspector of schools. I was speaking of the children's physical health, about their organism and what one could observe in it, and I told him about one child who has a heart disorder and another with some other disability and so on. Then the man exclaimed in astonishment, "But your teachers would need medical knowledge before this could be of any use in the school." Well, yes; if teachers need a certain amount of medical knowledge for a healthy education, then they must learn this. Life cannot be skewed to suit people's idiosyncrasies; we must establish our organization according to the requirements of life. Just as we must study before we can work in other areas, we must learn before we can do something in education.

Thus it is necessary, for example, that teachers see precisely all that takes place when a small child plays. Play involves a whole constellation of soul activities: joy, sometimes pain, sympathy, antipathy, and especially curiosity and a desire for knowledge. Children want to investigate the objects they play with and see what they are made of. When we observe this free and entirely spontaneous expression of soul—still unconstrained into any form of work—we must look at the shades of feeling and whether it is satisfying. When we guide children's play toward contentment, we improve their health by promoting an activity that is indirectly connected with the digestive system. And the way a person's play is guided during childhood can determine whether a person's blood circulation and digestive system become congested in old age. There is a delicate connection between the way a child plays and the growth and development of the physical organism.

One should not say that the physical organism is unimportant or claim to be an idealist and unconcerned with our lowly physical organism. The physical organism was brought into the world by divine spiritual powers; it is a divine creation, and we must understand that, as educators, we are called on to cooperate in this spiritual creation.

But I would rather express my meaning through a concrete example than use abstract statements. Suppose children show an extreme, pathological form of what we call a melancholic disposition; or imagine an extreme, pathological form of the sanguine temperament. The teacher must know where the border is between what is simply physical and what is pathological. If we see that a melancholic child is tending toward becoming pathological (and this happens far more often than one would think), we must contact the parents and inquire about the nature of the child's diet. We will discover a connection between that diet and the child's pathological melancholy. To give a concrete example (though there might be other causes), we will probably find that the child has been getting too little sugar at home. Because of this lack of sugar in the diet, the liver function is not regulated properly. A unique characteristic of melancholic children is that, whereas a certain substance, starch, is formed in the liver, it does not appear in the right amount. This substance may also to be found in plants. Everyone forms starch in the liver, but it is not the same as plant starch; it is an animal starch, which is transformed directly into sugar in the liver. The transformation of animal starch into sugar is a very important activity of the liver. In melancholic children, this does not function properly, and we must advise the parents to add sugar to their diet. In this way, we can regulate the liver's glycogenic function. You will see an extraordinary effect from this purely hygienic measure.

With sanguine children, you will find just the opposite; they are probably getting far too much sugar. They are given too many sweets and too much sugar in the diet. If they have developed a craving for sugar, in this case exactly the opposite liver activity will develop. The liver is an infinitely important organ, and it resembles a sense organ much more than one would imagine. The liver's purpose is to perceive the whole person from within, and it is vital to one's whole being. Thus, its organization differs from that of other organs. In other organs, a certain amount of arterial blood enters, and a certain amount of venous blood flows out. The liver, however, has an additional arrangement whereby a special vein enters and supplies the liver with extra venous blood. This has the effect of making the liver into a world of its own, so to speak—a world apart in the human being. It is this that enables us to perceive ourselves by means of the liver—that is, to perceive what affects our organism. The liver is an extremely fine barometer for sensing the sort of relationship human beings have with the outer world. You will effect an extraordinary improvement in pathologically sanguine children—those who are flighty and flit nervously from one thing to another—if you advise parents to diminish somewhat the amount of sugar in the diet. Thus, a real teacher can, even beyond the classroom time, provide guidance that will make children truly healthy, strong, and active in their physical functions. And you will notice how important this is for developing the whole human being.

Some of our most impressive experiences with children at the Waldorf school have been with those of fifteen or sixteen. We began with eight elementary classes, but we have added, class by class, the ninth, tenth, and now the eleventh. These upper classes, which are, of course, more advanced than the elementary classes, are made up of children of fifteen and sixteen, and they present certain difficulties. Some of these difficulties are of a soul and moral nature, which I will speak about later. But even in the physical sense, we find that human nature always tends toward the pathological and has to be protected from this.

Among girls, you might see a slight tendency toward chlorosis, or anemia, in the developing organism. The girl's blood becomes poor, and she becomes pale. This is because, from fourteen to sixteen, the spiritual nature becomes separated from the organism as a whole. And it is this spiritual nature that previously regulated the blood, but now the blood is left to itself. Consequently, it must be properly prepared so that its can accomplish this larger task on its own. Thus, girls are likely to become pale and anemic, and we must recognize this arises when we have failed to arouse a girl's interest in what we have been teaching or telling her. If attention and interest are kept alive, the whole physical organism participates in the activity, which engages the inmost self of the person, and thus anemia does not arise in the same way.[1]

The opposite is true for boys, who get a kind of neuritis, a condition in which there is too much blood in the brain. Therefore, during these years the brain acts as though it were congested with blood. In girls we find a lack of blood in the body; in boys an overabundance, especially in the head; there is too much white blood, the wrong form of venous and arterial blood. This occurs because the boys have been overstimulated; they have had to go quickly from one sensation to another without a break or proper rest. You will notice that even the troublesome behavior and difficulties among children of fourteen to sixteen are characteristic of this condition and are connected with physical development as a whole.

When we can view human nature in this way instead of denigrating the physical body, as teachers we can accomplish a great deal for the children's health. We must consider it a basic principle that spirituality becomes false as soon as it leads away from the material world to some castle in the clouds. If we denigrate the body because we consider it something low that must be suppressed, we will certainly not acquire the ability to educate in a healthy way. You see, you can forget about the physical

---

1. Chlorosis is also called greensickness, a benign type of iron-deficiency anemia in adolescent girls, marked by a pale yellow-green complexion.

body, and perhaps you can attain to a high state of abstraction in your spiritual nature, but it will be like a balloon flying away in the air. If spirituality is not connected to physical life, it cannot give anything to earthly social evolution. And before we can rise into the heavens, we must be prepared for the heavens, and this has to take place on earth. When people seek entry into heaven, they must pass the examination of death, and it is seldom the case in this materialistic time that people have spiritually nurtured the human physical organism, the highest creation of divine spiritual beings on earth. I will speak of the soul moral aspect in the next section, and on eurythmy following that.

There is much to do in the physical realm, apart from the educational measures in the school itself. And the same is true of the realms of soul and spirit. The important thing is to encourage people, even while in school, to find a proper entry into life. Again, I will illustrate the aim of the Waldorf school by concrete examples rather than abstract statements.

It is deemed necessary at the end of a school year to review the work of a child during the year. For us, it usually takes the form of a report on the child's progress and attainment in the various subjects in relation to the assigned work. In many countries, parents and guardians are told whether the children have met the standard by means of grades given as numbers, each indicating that a child has reached a certain proficiency in a given subject. Sometimes teachers are not certain that a 3 or 4 expresses the correct degree of achievement, so they write down 3½. Some teachers make a fine art of such calculation and even put down 3¼. I have to admit that I never acquired this fine art of expressing human abilities by using such numbers.

The Waldorf school reports are produced in a different way. If the college of teachers is unified to the degree that every child in the school is known to some degree by every teacher, it is possible to give a report that relates a child's whole nature.

Thus, our report on a child at the end of the school year resembles a short biography, an aperçu of one's experiences with that child during the year, both in and out of school. In this way, both the children and their parents or guardians have a reflection of what they are like at this age. At the Waldorf school, we have found that one can even put a severe reprimand into these mirror-like reports, and the children readily accept it.

We also write something else in these reports. We combine the past with the future. We know the children, and we know where they are deficient in volition, feeling, or thinking; we know when one emotion or another is uppermost. And in the light of this knowledge, we make a little verse, or saying, for each individual child in the Waldorf school, and we include it in their reports. It is meant to be a guiding thought for the whole next year at school. The children learn their verses by heart and keep them in mind. They work on the child's volition, emotions, or mental peculiarities, modifying and balancing them. Thus the report is not merely an intellectual expression of what the child has done, but it has a power itself and continues to work until the next report. We must indeed become familiar with the individuality of each child very accurately, as you will see, if we are to give such a potent report each year.

You can also see from this that our task in Waldorf education is not to establish schools that require exceptional external structure. We value the pedagogy and teaching, which can be introduced into any school. And we appreciate the influence that external conditions have on education in any school. We are not revolutionaries who simply say that city schools are useless and that schools should be out in the country and so on. On the contrary, we say that the conditions of life produce the situation, and we take the conditions as they exist. In every kind of school, we work for the welfare of humanity through a pedagogy that takes the given situation into account.

Working along these lines, it seems we can dispense with the the custom of holding some children back in the same class in an attempt to make them smarter. The Waldorf school has been criticized for having children in the upper classes whom the authorities judge should have been kept back. We find it exceedingly difficult, if only on humane grounds, to leave children behind; our teachers are so attached to their children that many tears would be shed if we had to do this. The truth is, an inner relationship arises between the children and teachers, and this is the real reason we can avoid the unhappy custom of holding children back. Besides, there is no real reason to keep children back. Suppose we hold a girl in back a previous class; that girl may be constituted in such a way that her mind develops in her eleventh year, and she would reach the class for eleven-year-old children a year too late. This causes much more harm than the possibility a teacher might encounter extra work because the girl has less understanding of the subjects, though she must nevertheless be taught with the others in the class.

The special class is reserved for children who are the slowest to develop. We have only one special class, which includes all the slowest children from the other classes. We have not had enough money for a variety of remedial classes, but this class has an exceptionally gifted teacher, Dr. Karl Schubert. When the question of establishing a special class came up, it was certainly obvious that he was the one to take this class. He has a special gift for it. He is able to make something of the pathological conditions of those children. He handles each child individually—so much so that he is happiest when he has them sitting around a table with him instead of on separate benches. The children who are slow of mind or have some other deficiency receive a treatment that enables them after a while to rejoin their classes.

Naturally this is a matter of time; but we transfer children to this class only rarely; and any time I find it necessary to transfer a child from a regular class into the special class, I first have to fight it out with the class teacher, who does not want to give up the child. Often it is a wonderful thing to see the deep relationship that has grown between the individual teachers and children. It means that this education is truly reaching the children's inner life.

It is all a matter of developing a method, for we are realistic, not some nebulous mystics. So, although we have had to make compromises with ordinary life, our method nevertheless makes it possible to bring out a child's individual disposition; at least, we have had many good results in the first few years. And because we have had to make compromises under present conditions, it has been impossible to give religious instruction to many of the children. We can, however, give them moral training, and we begin this with the feeling of gratitude.

Gratitude is a definite moral experience in relation to other human beings. Sentiments and notions that do not come out of gratitude lead to abstract precepts, at best, that regulate morality. But anything can come from gratitude, so from gratitude we develop the capacity for love and the feeling for duty. In this way, morality leads to religion. But outer circumstances have prevented us from joining those who would take the kingdom of heaven by storm, so we have handed over the instruction in Catholicism to the Catholic community, who send us a priest of their creed. Thus, the Catholic children are taught by a Catholic priest, and the evangelical Protestant children are taught by an evangelical pastor. The Waldorf school is not a school of life philosophy, but a means of education. It was discovered, however, that a certain number of children were dissenters and would receive no religious instruction under this arrangement.

As a result of the spirit that came into the Waldorf school, certain parents who otherwise would not have sent their children to a religion lesson ended up asking us to extend the teaching of morality into the area of religion. It therefore became necessary for us to give special religious instruction from the standpoint of spiritual science, or anthroposophy. Even in these religious lessons, we do not teach spiritual science but try to find symbols and parables in nature that lead toward religion. We try to bring the Gospels to the children in a way that will give them more spiritual understanding of religion and the like. Anyone who thinks the Waldorf school is a school for anthroposophy understands neither Waldorf education nor spiritual science.

Spiritual science truly arises from all the sciences and from life and did not need a name. But since this terrestrial world needs names for everything, it is called anthroposophy. But you cannot infer the scholar from the name, and similarly, just because we give anthroposophic religious instruction, you cannot assume that anthroposophy is introduced the way any other religious instruction might be from outside, as though it were a competing sect. How is spiritual science commonly understood? When people speak of it, they think of something sectarian, because at best they looked up the meaning of the word in the dictionary. This is like hearing the words "Max Miller from Oxford," and saying, "What sort of man is this? Perhaps a miller who bought corn and carted it to the mill to grind into flour and be delivered to the baker." Such a response to the name Miller would not say much about Max Miller, would it? The way people speak of anthroposophy, however, is just like this; it is like talking this way about Miller, spinning an opinion of anthroposophy based on the literal meaning of the word. People take it to be a sort of backwoods cult, whereas it is simply a fact that everything must have a name.

Indeed, I mean no offence in this, but others have made a great deal of it. The instruction in religion based on spiritual science is increasing, and more and more children come to it. Some have even deserted other religious instruction to go to the anthroposophic religious lessons. It is quite understandable, therefore, that people should say that these anthroposophists are rather bad people, since they lead children to abandon their Catholic and Protestant religious lessons for the religious instruction based on spiritual science. We do all we can to discourage them from coming, because it is very difficult for us to find religious teachers in our own area. Nevertheless, despite the fact that we never planned on this instruction except in response to parents' requests and the unconscious requests of children (to my great distress, I might almost say), the demand for anthroposophic religious instruction constantly increases. And now thanks to this anthroposophic religious instruction the school has a completely Christian character.

You can feel from the whole mood and being of the Waldorf school that a Christian quality pervades all the teaching and how religion is alive there, and this despite the fact that we never wanted to proselytize or connect the school with any church or sect. I have repeatedly said that the Waldorf principle does not establish a school to promote any particular philosophy of life, but to embody certain methods of education. Its goals are accomplished by a method based on knowledge of the human being. The goal itself is to help children become human beings who are sound in body, free in soul, and clear in spirit.

Now, let me say a little about the significance of teaching eurythmy and its value for children. To illustrate this, I would like to use these figures made in the Dornach studio. They are artistic representations of the essence of eurythmy. Their primary purpose is to help people appreciate artistic eurythmy, but I can also explain educational eurythmy with them.

Eurythmy is essentially visible speech; it is not mime or pantomime, nor is it an art form of dance.

When people sing or speak, they produce activity and movement in certain organs. The same movement that is inherent in the larynx and other speech organs can be extended and expressed in the whole human being. In our speech organs, movements are repressed and stopped. For example, an activity of the larynx that would manifest in this movement [representing "ah"], in which the wings of the larynx open out, is submerged in seed form. It becomes a movement into which the meaning of speech can be expressed, a movement that can then pass into the air and be heard. This is the original movement of "ah" [the letter *a*], the essential movement of the inner human being, so to speak. This is the movement that comes from the whole human being when expressing "ah." Thus, within every utterance of speech and song, there is an arrested movement in seed form. This seed wants to be expressed as movement by the whole human being. These are the forms of expression in movements, and they can be discovered.

The larynx and other organs take different forms for the sounds "ah," "ee," "l," and "m," and likewise there are corresponding movements and forms of movement. These forms of movement are the expressions of will that otherwise exist in expressions of thought and in the volition of speech and song. The abstract element of thought in speech is removed, and all intended expression is transformed into movement. Therefore, eurythmy is an art of movement in every sense. Just as you can hear "ah," you can also see it, and just as you can hear "ee," you can see it.

In these figures, the shapes in the wood are intended to express the movements. The figures are constructed on a three-color principle. The basic color expresses the form of the movement. Just as feeling pervades the tones of speech, feeling

Moral Teaching & Eurythmy in the Waldorf School

comes into the movement; we do not just speak a sound but also color it with feeling. We do this in eurythmy as well. In this way, a strong unconscious momentum plays into the eurythmy. If the eurythmist can bring this feeling into the movements in an artistic way, the audience will be affected by it as they watch.

Also keep in mind that the veil a eurythmist wears serves to enhance the expression of feeling; it accompanies and moves with the feeling. This was brought out in the performance [at Keble College]. You see here [in the figures] that the second color is mainly in the veils, representing the feeling nuance in the movement. Thus you have a first, fundamental color tht expresses the movement itself, and a second primarily in the veil placed over it, which expresses the feeling. The eurythmy performer must have the inner strength to express the feeling in movement. It is like the difference between ordering someone to do something and making a friendly request. It is in the nuance or level of feeling. Just as an order is different from a request, this second color—expressed here as blue on a foundation of green—continues into the veil. This represents the feeling nuance in the language of eurythmy.

The third aspect that is brought out is character, or a strong element of volition. This can be introduced into eurythmy only when a performer can experience the movements as they are made, thus giving them strong expression. The way performers position the head as they do eurythmy makes a great difference in the way they appear. Whether, for example, one keeps the muscles on the left of the head taut and those on the right relaxed—this is expressed here [in another figure] by means of a third color. You see the muscles on the left of the head are somewhat tense, those on the right relaxed. Observe how the third color always indicates this here. You see the left side contracted, and down over the mouth. Here [in another figure] the muscles of the forehead are contracted. This, you see, sets the tone of the whole inner character; it radiates from this slight contraction, for this slight contraction radiates throughout the organism. Thus the art of eurythmy is really composed of movement, expressed in the fundamental color; the feeling nuance, expressed by the second color; and volition. Indeed, volition is the basis of the whole art, but emphasized in a special way.

When the intention is to exhibit the features of eurythmy, only those parts only of the human being are selected that characterize eurythmy. If we had figures here with beautifully painted noses and eyes and beautiful mouths, they might be charming, but for eurythmy this is not the point; what you see painted, shaped, or carved here belongs solely to the art of eurythmy in the performer.

A eurythmy performer does not need to make any particular facial expression; it doesn't matter. It goes without saying, of course, that a normal, healthy eurythmist would not make a disagreeable facial expression while performing a friendly gesture, just as one would not do when speaking. There is no goal of artistic facial expression independent of eurythmic expression. For example, a performer can perform the gesture for *a* by rotating the eyes outward; this is allowed and in keeping with eurythmy. But it would not be appropriate to make dramatic, sweeping gestures, as one does in mime. Though often required especially in mime, when performing eurythmy they would merely be distortions of expression. In eurythmy, everything must have the quality of eurythmy. So, here we have a form of art that demonstrates only the part of the human being that is eurythmy; everything else is eliminated. Thus we get an artistic impression, for each art must express only what is appropriate through its own special medium. A statue cannot be made to speak, so you must bring out the desired expression of soul through the shape of the mouth and face. Neither would it have worked here [in the eurythmy figures] to paint human performers in a naturalistic way; they had to be painted as immediate expressions of eurythmy.

Naturally, when I speak of veils, I do not mean that one will be able change the veil with each letter expressed. One can find the mood of the poem, however, by trying the various feeling nuances for a poem as a whole, by entering its mood, which might be a feeling of the letter *a* or perhaps *b*. Thus one can perform the whole poem correctly using a single veil. The same is true for color. I have established the veil form, color, and so on that may be combined for each letter. There must be a certain essential key in a poem, and this is provided by the color of the veil and, in general, by the color combination as a whole. This must be retained throughout the poem, otherwise the performers would have to continually change veils. They would constantly throw off veils and change dresses, and matters would be even more complicated than they already are—and people would understand even less. In fact, however, once one has the fundamental key, it can be maintained throughout the entire poem, using only the movements themselves to express changes in letters, syllables, and moods.

Now, since my aim today relates to education, I have arranged these figures according to the order in which children learn the sounds. The first sound they learn, while still quite young, is the sound "ah" [the letter *a*]. Then they continue approximately in this order, for naturally when children are involved there are many digressions. On the whole, however, the children learn the vowels in this order: *a, e, i. o, u*—the usual order. Then, when the children practice the visible speech of eurythmy, they come to do it in this order. And, for them, it is like a memory of what they felt when first learning the sounds of speech as little children—a rebirth at another level. In the language of eurythmy, children experience what they experienced earlier. It affirms the power of the word in them through the medium of their whole being.

Then the children learn the consonants in this order: *m, b, p, d, t, l, n*. There should also be an "ng" sound here, as in *sing*, but it has not yet been made. Then the letters *f, h, g, s, r*. That mysterious letter *r* has three proper forms in human speech, and it is the last one that children perfect. There is a lip *r*, a palatal *r*, and an *r* spoken in the back of the mouth.[2] Thus, in speech and in the organ of speaking or singing, children learn something that can be taken into their whole being and developed as visible speech.

If there is sufficient interest for this expressive art, we could make more figures—for example, figures for joy, sorrow, antipathy, sympathy, and other feelings that are all part of eurythmy. And it is not just grammar, but prose also comes into its own in eurythmy. We could make figures for all these; then people could see how this spiritual-soul activity has a definite value both in education and as an art, since soul activity not only influences the the way our physical body functions, but also develops our soul and physical organic nature. As for these eurythmy figures, they also serve in the study of eurythmy as a aid to the memory of our students. Do not imagine that eurythmy is easy and can be learned in a few hours; a eurythmist requires thorough training. Thus, these figures are also used by eurythmy students to help them go more deeply into their art. You can see there is much contained in the forms themselves, though they are carved and painted quite simply.

Today, I wanted to speak of the art of eurythmy insofar as it forms part of the educational principle of the Waldorf school.

---

2. This guttural *r* is characterized by a sound articulated in the back of the mouth, as the non-English velar fricative sound "kh."

Teachers in the Waldorf School

August 25, 1922

Yesterday I alluded to the events that take place when boys and girls reach puberty at fourteen or fifteen. At this stage, the teachers who are serious about their responsibilities will face numerous difficulties. Such difficulties are especially obvious in a school or college in which education is derived from human nature. Overcoming these difficulties by extraneous discipline is not an option, because if they are repressed now they will merely reappear later on in life in all sort of other forms. It is far better to face these problems squarely as inherent to human nature and deal with them. In a Waldorf school, where boys and girls are educated together and keep constant company with one another, these difficulties occur frequently.

We have already spoken of the difference between boys and girls, and this begins to appear around the tenth year. Girls at this age begin to grow more quickly, especially in height. Boys' growth is delayed until around puberty, and then boys catch up with the girls. This fact is very significant for those who observe the fine interplay of spirit, soul, and body from the standpoint of true human knowledge. Growth, which means overcoming earth's gravity, engages one's essential being, whereas one is not really concerned about whether a certain organic phenomenon appears at one stage or another in life. In fact, there are certain cosmic, suprasensory influences that work on human beings from the external world, and these affect the female organization more intensely between the tenth and twelfth years than they do the male organism. In a sense, females during this time even physically partake of the suprasensory world.

Please realize the significance of this. Between perhaps the tenth and fourteenth years, the female organization begins to live more in a spiritual element; it is permeated by spirit at this time, and this affects the blood processes of girls in a very special way. During this time, the blood circulation is, in a sense, in contact with the whole universe. Its time must come from the universe and be regulated by it. If we were to perform experiments to determine the relationship between the rhythms of blood and breathing during this period of growth—even using physical instruments—we would find this relationship stronger among girls than boys.

Boys of thirteen or fourteen begin to show a nature thus far hidden. They also begin to grow more quickly than do girls. And they grow in all directions, making up for the delayed growth. At the same time, boys' relationship to the outer world is quite different than it was during earlier periods of life. And so, in boys it is now the nervous system that is affected rather than the blood circulation. Thus, it can easily happen that a boy's nervous system gets overtaxed if school instruction is not given in the right way. For, during these years, the form and meaning of the language or languages he has learned have an enormous influence. The human ideas enshrined in language—whether his first or second language—press in upon and beset him, as it were, as his body grows more delicate. Thus, within boys at this age, the whole world drones and surges—that is, the world of their earthly environment.

In girls, a year or two earlier, something of the surrounding universe is planted in them. In boys, the earthly environment is planted in them through the medium of language. This is obviously externally in a boy's change of voice. And indirectly connected with this vocal transformation, enormously important events take place in a boy's whole organism. In the female organism, the voice is rounded off in a very slight way. On the other hand, connected with a girl's quickened growth, a preparation has taken place in the organism, involving the flow of heavenly realms into the young woman. Recent advances in materialistic science are confirmed by a spiritual view.

You see, when people hear that spiritual views or values are confirmed, they are likely to say, "Those oddball cranks dismiss everything earthly and material." And then a natural scientist comes along and cites the marvelous advances of purely material science in recent centuries. And so people believe that anyone who advocates something so alien as spiritual science is unconcerned with material things or practical life. And I am not saying that anthroposophy is alien to the world, but that the world is alien to anthroposophy. But it is precisely spiritual science that takes up the latest discoveries of the natural sciences with immense love and saturates them with knowledge from the spiritual world. Consequently, it is precisely among those who support spiritual philosophy that there is a true appreciation of materialism. A spiritualist can afford to be a materialist, but a pure materialist lacks knowledge of matter by having lost the spirit; only the outer appearance of matter can be observed. It is the materialist who lacks real insight into material processes. I point this out, because it seems very significant to me.

Consider a Waldorf teacher's attitude toward children; here you have a very different perspective of children who have reached puberty—children who have just passed through a stage of development that includes the organic changes I spoke of earlier. They see these in a different way than do those who know nothing of this from the spiritual point of view.

A boy of fourteen or fifteen echoes the surrounding world in his being. That is, words and their meaning are taken unconsciously into his nervous system, and they echo in his nerves. The boy doesn't know what to do with himself. Something enters him and begins to feel foreign at this age; he is confused by himself and feels irresponsible. Those who understand human nature know very well that this two-legged being of earth called "anthropos" is never—not even to a philosopher—a greater mystery than to a fifteen year old boy. At this age, all the human soul forces are beset by mystery. In a boy of fifteen or sixteen, human volition, the capacity most remote from normal consciousness, begins to assault the nervous system.

It is different for girls, but we should aim at equal treatment and recognition for both sexes, which must come in the future. Nevertheless, is all the more important to distinguish clearly between the sexes. Whereas for a boy, his self becomes a perplexing problem, for girls at this age the problem is the world around them. Girl take into themselves something other than earth. A girl's whole nature develops unconsciously within her. A girl of fourteen or fifteen is a being who faces the world with a sense of amazement, finding it full of problems. She is, above all, a being who looks to the world for ideals to live by. Thus, much in the outer world becomes enigmatic to girls at this age. To a boy, the inner world presents many enigmas. To a girl, it is the outer world. We must understand and feel that we are now dealing with very new children; they are not the same children we had before. In some cases, the change arrives remarkably fast, and teachers who are not alive to the transformation may not perceive that they are suddenly confronted by a whole new person.

This is why a most essential aspect in Waldorf teacher training involves receptivity to changes in human nature. And the teachers have acquired this relatively quickly, for reasons I will explain. A Waldorf teacher must be prepared to face something that will be completely different tomorrow from what it was yesterday. This is the true secret of teacher training. For example, in the evening we usually think that tomorrow the sun will rise and things will be pretty much the same as they were today. Now, to use a somewhat extreme notion to express my meaning, Waldorf teachers must be prepared for tomorrow, whether the sun rises or not. Unless our view of human nature is as fresh as this, without preconceptions from the past, we cannot comprehend human growth and development. We may rest assured that changes out in the cosmos will be somewhat conservative, but when it comes to transitions in human nature, from early childhood to the teens, then, ladies and gentlemen, the sun that rose before may not come up again. In this human microcosm, *anthropos,* such a great change occurs that we face an entirely new situation. It's as though nature one day confronts us with a world of darkness in which our eyes have became useless.

We need open minds, ready to receive new wisdom each day, and a disposition that can transform accumulated knowledge into a sense of potential that leaves the mind clear for the new. This keeps people healthy, fresh, and active. A heart that is open to changes in life—its unexpected and continuous freshness—must be a Waldorf teacher's basic mood and nature.

This change significantly affects the relationship between boys and girls at this age and their teachers. This was demonstrated last year by an episode at the school. One day I was back again at the Waldorf school to direct the education there (something I can do only occasionally), and a girl in the top class came to me between lessons. I would say that her mood was one of suppressed aggression. She was very emotional, but with extraordinary inner determination she said to me, "May we speak to you today? It is very urgent. The whole class would like to speak with you today, but only if you wish it." You see, she had made herself class leader and wanted to speak with me in the presence of the whole class. What was her reason? The boys and girls had begun to feel that they had lost touch with the teachers. They found it difficult to connect with the teachers in the right way.

This was not caused by any hard feelings toward the teachers. There is no grudge among the children against the teachers of the school. On the contrary, during the short time the school has existed, they have come to love their teachers. But these children of fifteen and sixteen were now terribly afraid that they might lose this love because of the new relationship that had arisen between the students and teachers; they had an extraordinary fear of this. I did not snub them and put them in their places, as might have been done in the past if children blurted out this sort of thing; rather, I went to meet and speak to the children. At this age, of course, one should call them young ladies and gentlemen, as I said before. I spoke to them in a way that made them realize I was prepared then and there to discuss the matter and reach a conclusion with them. I said, "We can discuss this together without restraint and resolve it once we discover the problem."

Then, what I have just described came out—tremendous anxiety over the possibility of being unable to love the teachers as they had before. Enormous wonder and curiosity about certain worldly matters had entered the children. And since Waldorf pedagogy is evolved day by day, each event must be studied carefully, with educational measures based on living experience. The children said much that had little to do the issue, but it seemed immensely important to them, and they felt it deeply. Then I said a good many things to them about how we discover this or that in life as time goes on, and the children eagerly agreed. It turned out that all we needed was to rearrange the teachers slightly for the following school year.

At the beginning of the following school year, I assigned language teaching to a different teacher. I just shuffled the teachers a bit. Further, we realized in the college of teachers that this was the method we should use throughout the school—that we should make decisions by working with the students. But before one could accept this new situation—that is, meeting with young ladies and gentlemen of this age on equal terms, whereas one was previously an authority—it is essential to have what the Waldorf teachers have: an open worldview. In German, we call this a *Weltanschauung* [an ideology]. One does not merely train in a teaching method; we must also have our own ideas concerning the destiny of humanity, the significance of historical epochs, the meaning of present life, and so on. These questions must not buzz around in one's head, but remain in one's heart. Then one will have a heartfelt experience of these matters while in the company of children.

During the past four or five hundred years of western civilization, we have entered deeply into intellectualism; this however is unnoticed by the majority of people. Intellectualism, however, is naturally suited only to older people, whereas children are naturally averse to this mind-set. Nevertheless, all modern thinking is tinged with intellectualism. Thus far, the only people who have not yet become intellectual are those over in Asia and in Russia, as far as Moscow. West of Moscow and as far as America, intellectualism is universal. We remain unaware of this, but to the degree that we belong to the so-called cultured classes, we think in a kind of mental language that children cannot understand. This accounts for today's chasm between adults and children. This chasm must be filled by teachers such as we have in a Waldorf school. This can be done only when we are able to see deeply into human nature.

Allow me to say something of a physiological nature, something not usually considered. It can be correctly appreciated only when we encounter it as a fact of spiritual science. People believe it is a great accomplishment when something is formed as a concept. But only those who assess everything in their heads believe this, and truths are often very contradictory. If we go into the unconscious and our feeling nature, we find that all ideas, even those of philosophers, are connected to a slight feeling of antipathy. There is something distasteful in the formulation of ideas, whether we are aware of it or not. Thus, it is enormously important not to accentuate this subconscious distaste in children by giving them too many concepts and ideas.

This arises from the fact that when someone has been thinking very hard, the inside of the brain presents a strange formation. Unfortunately, I can give you only the facts on this, since it would take many lectures to demonstrate how it works physiologically. The brain is permeated by deposits of phosphorus compounds, deposited in the process of thinking. This is especially true when thinking one's own thoughts. The brain becomes filled with unreason (pardon the word); it fills with deposited products such as phosphoric acid compounds, which litter the brain. These excretions are removed from the organism only when we sleep or relax. Consequently, the process that accompanies thought is not one of growth or digestion; it is a catabolic process that breaks down substances. When I follow a train of thought of someone who is somewhat mature—say, over sixteen years old—I set up a catabolic process that leaves deposits. It is this elimination of substance that provides the foundation for self-awareness.

Now if I simply dictate ideas, on the other hand, by stating finite concepts that have been formulated dogmatically, I put a person into a peculiar state. Finite concepts cannot take hold in human nature. They jostle and press one another and find no entry to the brain; instead they beat against the brain and cause it to use up old deposited substances through its nerve activity.

The effect of finite intellectual concepts is to compel us to recycle the discarded substances that lie about within us. This gives us a feeling of slight distaste, which remains subconscious as it influences our disposition all the more. You see, unless we recognize these facts, we cannot appreciate their importance. People do not realize that thinking breaks down substance or that thinking in mere ideas forces us to reuse what we have thrown off; we rehash the cast-off phosphoric acid salts.

This is extremely important when applied to moral education. If we give children definite precepts as concepts, we cause them approach morality in terms of ideas, and thus antipathy arises. The inner human organism rebels against and fights abstract moral precepts or commandments. On the other hand, I can encourage children to form their own moral feelings directly from life and from example, and this leads them to the catabolic stage. We get them to formulate moral principles as free, autonomous human beings. In this way, I help children toward an activity that benefits their entire being. If I merely give children moral precepts, I make morality distasteful to them, and this plays an important role in modern society. It's difficult to imagine the degree of disgust people feel toward some of the most beautiful and noblest of human moral impulses, simply because they were given in the form of precepts and intellectual ideas.

Waldorf teachers learn these things through spiritual science. Indeed, it is this that gives them insight into such material processes. Let me say it again; materialism assumes the appropriate place in life only when we view it from the standpoint of spirit. This provides an understanding of what really takes place in the human being. Only by adopting a spiritual standpoint can we become truly practical educators in the physical world. But this is possible only when teachers themselves have a philosophy of life—when their view of the world causes them to feel the deep meaning of the question of the universe and human destiny.

Again I must make an abstract statement, but really it is very concrete; it only seems abstract. You see, as human beings we confront the mystery of the universe, and we look for a solution to our questions. People today, however, assume that the solution to this mystery can be written out in a book and expressed in the form of ideas. Keep in mind, however, that there are those—and I have met a few—who have an extreme fear of a solution to the mystery of the universe. They claim that, if such a solution were discovered and written in a book, what in the world would those who come after them have to do? They would be extremely bored. All the elements of a solution are available and need only to be understood. People think this would be truly boring, and I don't really blame them; the world really would be a boring place if someone wrote a book containing the answer to the mystery of the universe once and for all. We could simply read the book, and then what would in fact remain for us to do in this world?

But we do not understand the human being as we should. We must start at the beginning, and humankind is an answer that takes us back to the beginning. And we must come to know this answer to our question: the human being, this Oedipus. And this causes us to reexperience the mystery of our own inner self. Every new human being is a fresh problem to be understood. You see, there must be something in existence that, once we have the key, calls us to greater effort toward a so-called solution. The mystery of the universe should not be stated as something to be solved once and for all. Instead, the solution should give us the energy to make a fresh start. And if universal questions are understood correctly, this is what happens. The world presents us with many questions—so many, in fact, that we cannot even perceive them all. By "questions" I do not only mean those matters for which there are abstract answers. I mean questions about what we will do—the actions that result from our volition and feelings—and about all the many details of life. This is what I mean when I say the world presents us with numerous questions. So what is the real answer to these myriad questions? It is really the human being. The world is full of mysteries, and people confront them. Human beings are a synthesis and a summary, and the answer to the mystery of the universe comes from the human being.

If one wants to become a Waldorf teacher, it means working from a true philosophy of life, and this mysterious relationship between the human being and the cosmos must become an unconscious wisdom of one's feelings. People today become alarmed if someone says that Waldorf teachers begin with spiritual science, which gives them their vision. What if this anthroposophy is imperfect? This is possible, so why not produce philosophies you think are better? A philosophy is needed for those who must work with human beings as an artist. And this is what teaching involves.

When I look back over these nine lectures, I find much to criticize as imperfect, but my greatest regret is that I gave them in the form I did. I would have much preferred not to give these lectures at all, as contradictory as this may sound. These lectures have been too much in keeping with the spirit of the time. For it seems to me that there is an incredible amount of discussion about the nature of education in our age—far too much. People seem far too driven to discuss the issue of how we should educate. And when we have to go into these questions ourselves, though from a different view, one realizes how it is all just too much.

But why is there so much talk about education today? Almost every little town you come to announces lectures on how to educate. How does it come about that there is so much discussion and so many conferences and talks everywhere on this subject? If we look back to earlier ages of human history, we do not find that people talked nearly so much about education. It was something people did innocently by instinct, and they knew what they were doing.

I have said that a truly healthy education must be based on a knowledge of the human being, and that the staff of the Waldorf school must acquire this knowledge in the way I have described. So it is worth asking how those of earlier ages understood the human being so much better than we do. As strange as it may seem, we can answer that the people of previous ages were not as enlightened as we are in the area of natural science. But, in their own way, they knew more about the human being than we do. I mentioned before in these lectures that humankind has gradually come to be considered a final product. We look at all the other creatures in the world and claim that they evolved up to the human being, the final product. And this is where we stop, having very little to say about the actual human being. Modern physiology even tries explain the human being by experimenting on animals. We have lost the ability to give humankind as such a real place in the world. To a large extent, we have lost the human as a being.

Spiritual science tries to reclaim knowledge of the world that does not exclude the human being. Such knowledge does not view the human being as merely the latest organism. With this knowledge of the world, one gains the power to see into the real nature of the human being as soul, body, and spirit. Further, one is able to comprehend what spirit actually does in the human being, and how the intellectual form of spirit breaks down substances, as I described. Our current way of viewing history does not achieve this; it halts with the human being, who is lumped together with animals. A biology is formulated, and this is connected with physiology, but there is no grasp of what the human being really is. As a result, people today act a great deal out of instinct, but as an object of scientific knowledge, the human being is not viewed favorably.

Teachers require a science that will once again enable them to love the human being, because they can first love their own knowing. There is much wisdom behind the fact that people of ancient times did not simply speak about acquiring knowledge; they spoke of *philo sophia*, a love of wisdom. *Anthropos sophia*, anthroposophy, would have human beings once again acquire wisdom that leads to a knowledge of the human being.

When all knowledge and science centers on the human being, then we can answer educational questions through every aspect of our philosophy. All the knowledge we need, even about children, can be found everywhere. This is what we need. Because ordinary science tells us nothing about education, we create extra institutions and talk too much about education. Lectures such as these will achieve their object only when they have become superfluous—that is, when there is no longer any need to treat this as a special theme; when we once again possess a worldview in which education is implicit; when teacher have this knowledge and possess the art of education that they can exercise spontaneously. Our need to talk so much about education shows how little the rest of our knowledge involves an impulse for education. We need a complete change of direction.

This is the real reason why Waldorf teachers do not cultivate a special pedagogy but cultivate a philosophy of life. By teaching them to understand the human being, it is possible for them to be spontaneous and naive again in education. And this explains why, when speaking of Waldorf teachers, we must speak of the whole human being. This also eliminates the possiblity of being fanatical about Waldorf education. Fanaticism, which is so rife among people today, is ruled out here. Fanaticism is the worst thing in the world, especially in education. It causes people to push ahead in one direction, regardless of anything but a single goal reduced to precise slogans.

If, however, we look at the world without preconceptions, we will agree that views and opinions are no more than views and opinions. If I photograph a tree, I have one view of it; this view shows a definite form, but the view is different from somewhere else, and different again from over another place. You might even think it was not the same tree if you had only the pictures to judge by. Likewise, there are various points of view in the world, each regarding only one aspect. If you know that things must be seen from manifold positions, you can avoid fanaticism and live in universality.

Ladies and gentlemen, you will find goodness everywhere by simply realizing that most of what people say is not wrong, but lopsided. One merely needs to consider the other view and see the other side. Consequently, it is so strange if one is talking about Waldorf education, and someone says, of course, we do this already, but so-and-so does it all wrong. And then so-and-so says, we do this, but they do it very poorly. A Waldorf teacher would say they have their good points and so-and-so also has good points; we try to use what we find to be universal. This is why we often hear, Waldorf education says the same things we say. This is not so, however; rather, we say things that others can then agree with, because we understand that a fanatical pursuit of one line works the greatest damage. It is essential for Waldorf teachers to be free of all fanaticism and confront only the reality of the growing child.

It is true that many people may claim to have encountered many fanatics in the anthroposophic movement. But if they look at things more closely, they will find that the goal of spiritual science is to make knowledge universal and to spiritualize it. It is a matter of indifference that it is called anthroposophy, as I explained. In fact, its only object is to universalize what has become lopsided. If people have found fanaticism and dogmatism within the anthroposophic movement, this came from outside; it is not inherent in the movement. Much is carried into the movement that does not accord with its nature and being. Consequently, when someone says that there is some sort of cult behind Waldorf education, one in which people indulge all kinds of crazes, that individual should study the matter properly and discover what it is a Waldorf school lives by. Then one will see that spiritual science can indeed give life to education and that, far from pursuing anything outlandish or falsely idealistic, it wishes only to realize the human ideal in living human beings.

I will close these lectures by saying that the life speaking through Waldorf teachers arises from this source. Let me add that, although I said that I regretted the need to give these lectures, it has nevertheless been a great joy to me to give them. I thank this honorable audience for the attention and interest you have shown.

The Foundations
of Waldorf Education

THE FIRST FREE WALDORF SCHOOL opened in Stuttgart in September 1919 under the auspices of Emil Molt, director of the Waldorf Astoria Cigarette Company and a student of Rudolf Steiner's spiritual science, and particularly of Steiner's call for social renewal.

It was only the previous year—amid the social chaos following the end of World War I—that Molt, responding to Steiner's prognosis that truly human change would not be possible unless a sufficient number of people received an education that developed the whole human being, decided to create a school for his workers' children. Conversations with the minister of education and with Steiner, in early 1919, then led rapidly to the forming of the first school.

Since that time, more than six hundred schools have opened around the globe—from Italy, France, Portugal, Spain, Holland, Belgium, Britain, Norway, Finland, and Sweden to Russia, Georgia, Poland, Hungary, Romania, Israel, South Africa, Australia, Brazil, Chile, Peru, Argentina, Japan, and others—making the Waldorf school movement the largest independent school movement in the world. The United States, Canada, and Mexico alone now have more than 120 schools.

Although each Waldorf school is independent, and although there is a healthy oral tradition going back to the first Waldorf teachers and to Steiner himself, as well as a growing body of secondary literature, the true foundations of the Waldorf method and spirit remain the many lectures that Steiner gave on the subject. For five years (1919–1924) Steiner worked simultaneously on many other fronts, tirelessly dedicating himself to the dissemination of Waldorf educational ideas. He gave numerous lectures to teachers, parents, children, and the public. New schools were established and the movement grew.

Whereas many of Steiner's foundational lectures have been translated and published, some have never appeared in English, and many have been difficult to obtain for many years. To establish a coherent basis for Waldorf education, SteinerBooks is publishing the complete series of Steiner's lectures and writings on education. *The Foundations of Waldorf Education* constitutes an authoritative ground for efforts toward educational renewal, for Waldorf teachers, parents, and educators in general.

Rudolf Steiner's Lectures and Writings on Education

I. *Allgemeine Menschenkunde als Grundlage der Pädagogik: Pädagogischer Grundkurs,* 14 lectures, Stuttgart, 1919 (GA 293). Previously *Study of Man.* **The Foundations of Human Experience** (Anthroposophic Press, 1996).

II. *Erziehungskunst Methodische-Didaktisches,* 14 lectures, Stuttgart, 1919 (GA 294). **Practical Advice to Teachers** (Rudolf Steiner Press, 1988).

III. *Erziehungskunst,* 15 discussions, Stuttgart, 1919 (GA 295). **Discussions with Teachers** (Anthroposophic Press, 1997).

IV. *Die Erziehungsfrage als soziale Frage,* 6 lectures, Dornach, 1919 (GA 296). Previously *Education as a Social Problem.* **Education as a Force for Social Change** (Anthroposophic Press, 1997).

V. *Die Waldorf Schule und ihr Geist,* 6 lectures, Stuttgart and Basel, 1919 (GA 297). **The Spirit of the Waldorf School** (Anthroposophic Press, 1995).

VI. *Rudolf Steiner in der Waldorfschule, Vorträge und Ansprachen,* 24 lectures and conversations and one essay, Stuttgart, 1919–1924 (GA 298). **Rudolf Steiner in the Waldorf School: Lectures and Conversations** (Anthroposophic Press, 1996).

VII. *Geisteswissenschaftliche Sprachbetrachtungen,* 6 lectures, Stuttgart, 1919 (GA 299). **The Genius of Language** (Anthroposophic Press, 1995).

VIII. *Konferenzen mit den Lehrern der Freien Waldorfschule 1919–1924,* 3 volumes (GA 300a–c). **Faculty Meetings with Rudolf Steiner,** 2 volumes (Anthroposophic Press, 1998).

IX. *Die Erneuerung der pädagogisch-didaktischen Kunst durch Geisteswissenschaft,* 14 lectures, Basel, 1920 (GA 301). **The Renewal of Education** (Anthroposophic Press, 2001).

X. *Menschenerkenntnis und Unterrichtsgestaltung*, 8 lectures, Stuttgart, 1921 (GA 302). Previously *The Supplementary Course: Upper School* and *Waldorf Education for Adolescence*. ***Education for Adolescents*** (Anthroposophic Press, 1996).

XI. *Erziehung und Unterricht aus Menschenerkenntnis*, 9 lectures, Stuttgart, 1920, 1922, 1923 (GA 302a). The first four lectures are in ***Balance in Teaching*** (Mercury Press, 1982); last three lectures in ***Deeper Insights into Education*** (Anthroposophic Press, 1988).

XII. *Die gesunde Entwicklung des Menschenwesens,* 16 lectures, Dornach, 1921–22 (GA 303). ***Soul Economy: Body, Soul, and Spirit in Waldorf Education*** (Anthroposophic Press, 2003).

XIII. *Erziehungs- und Unterrichtsmethoden auf anthroposophischer Grundlage*, 9 public lectures, various cities, 1921–22 (GA 304). ***Waldorf Education and Anthroposophy 1*** (Anthroposophic Press, 1995).

XIV. *Anthroposophische Menschenkunde und Pädagogik,* 9 public lectures, various cities, 1923–24 (GA 304a). ***Waldorf Education and Anthroposophy 2*** (Anthroposophic Press, 1996).

XV. *Die geistig-seelischen Grundkräfte der Erziehungskunst,* 12 Lectures, 1 special lecture, Oxford, 1922 (GA 305). ***The Spiritual Ground of Education*** (Anthroposophic Press, 2004).

XVI. *Die pädagogische Praxis vom Gesichtspunkte geisteswissenschaftlicher Menschenerkenntnis,* 8 lectures, Dornach, 1923 (GA 306). ***The Child's Changing Consciousness as the Basis of Pedagogical Practice*** (Anthroposophic Press, 1996).

XVII. *Gegenwärtiges Geistesleben und Erziehung,* 14 lectures, Ilkeley, 1923 (GA 307). ***A Modern Art of Education*** (Anthroposophic Press, 2004) and ***Education and Modern Spiritual Life*** (Garber Publications, 1989).

XVIII. *Die Methodik des Lehrens und die Lebensbedingungen des Erziehens*, 5 lectures, Stuttgart, 1924 (GA 308). ***The Essentials of Education*** (Anthroposophic Press, 1997).

XIX. *Anthroposophische Pädagogik und ihre Voraussetzungen,* 5 lectures, Bern, 1924 (GA 309). *The Roots of Education* (Anthroposophic Press, 1997).

XX. *Der pädagogische Wert der Menschenerkenntnis und der Kulturwert der Pädagogik,* 10 public lectures, Arnheim, 1924 (GA 310). *Human Values in Education* (Rudolf Steiner Press, 1971).

XXI. *Die Kunst des Erziehens aus dem Erfassen der Menschenwesenheit,* 7 lectures, Torquay, 1924 (GA 311). *The Kingdom of Childhood* (Anthroposophic Press, 1995).

XXII. *Geisteswissenschaftliche Impulse zur Entwicklung der Physik. Erster naturwissenschaftliche Kurs: Licht, Farbe, Ton—Masse, Elektrizität, Magnetismus,* 10 lectures, Stuttgart, 1919–20 (GA 320). *The Light Course* (Anthroposophic Press, 2001).

XXIII. *Geisteswissenschaftliche Impulse zur Entwicklung der Physik. Zweiter naturwissenschaftliche Kurs: die Wärme auf der Grenze positiver und negativer Materialität,* 14 lectures, Stuttgart, 1920 (GA 321). *The Warmth Course* (Mercury Press, 1988).

XXIV. *Das Verhältnis der verschiedenen naturwissenschaftlichen Gebiete zur Astronomie. Dritter naturwissenschaftliche Kurs: Himmelskunde in Beziehung zum Menschen und zur Menschenkunde,* 18 lectures, Stuttgart, 1921 (GA 323). Available in typescript only as **"The Relation of the Diverse Branches of Natural Science to Astronomy."**

XXV. *The Education of the Child and Early Lectures on Education* (a collection; Anthroposophic Press, 1996).

XXVI. Miscellaneous.

Index

A

acquisitiveness, 72–73
active principle, 24
activity, 18
adding, leading to desiring and craving, 72–73
Allbutt, Clifford, 49
anemia, 108
anger, removing from children, 78
animal kingdom, 76
    study of, 68–69
    synthesis of the human being, 68–69
anthropology, 3
anthropomorphism, 63
anthroposophy, 114–15, 123, 134–35
appearance, experiencing world of, 23
arithmetic, 70–73
art, effect on rhythmic system, 50–51
artistic patterns, 102–3
asceticism, 28–31, 32
authority
    children's reliance on, 33
    gradual change to looking for, 58
    principle of, 9–10

B

biography, 76
birth, existence before, 3
blessing, power of, 12
blood system, 7, 76
    in pubescent girls, 122
    related to feeling, 38–39, 45
blushing, 39, 42
bodily life, 13
body
    avoiding transparency of, 29–30
    constraining to become transparent to world of spirit, 32
    eliminating, 28–29
    keeping from being a hindrance to the spirit, 49
    progressing from soul into spirit, 37
    reaching through soul and spirit, 74
botany, 66–68
boys, 109, 122–24
brain
    effects of exposure to finite concepts on, 128–29
    effects of hard thinking on, 128
    hardening, 77
    uniting breathing with, 21
breathing, 21, 38–39, 45

C

carving, 97–99, 103
causality, understanding of, 75–76
chemistry, 75
children
    becoming followers, 10
    body as witness to spiritual worlds, 333
    critical point of development, 11
    developing, 59
    difficult, 55
    dominance of sensory activity and effect on breathing, 50
    fundamentally different at various life stages, 6
    hidden intelligence of, 26
    idea development of, 11–12
    as imitators, 6, 46
    inability to distinguish between internal and external, 63
    inspiration ruling, 13
    instinctive interaction with teachers, 9–10
    liveliness in, 77–78
    living outside themselves, 7–8
    moving from sense organ to soul, 10
    observing, 5
    preferred method of teaching, 10
    preparing for adulthood, 12
    presenting with images rather than logic, 34
    proletarian, 90
    recognizing threefold system in, 50
    revealing spiritual divine matters, 55
    reverence toward, 55
    as sense organs, 6–9, 41, 45
    soul development of, 11–12
    spirit and soul in, 6, 16
    taste in, 41–42
    teaching through imagery, 25–26
    temperaments of, 80–83
    thankfulness for, 54
    working with soul, 37–38
chlorosis, 108
choleric children, 82, 83
clairvoyance, approaching through soul-spiritual methods, 30–31
clear thinking, 31
coeducation, 100, 121–22
cognition, applying forces to observing human being, 5
color
    in eurythmy, 117, 119
    experience of, 101–2, 104
    special attention given to, 85–86
commands, ineffectiveness of, 52
consonants, 16–17, 120
counting, arbitrariness of, 71
cuneiform, 59

D

death, existence after, 3
digestive system, play indirectly connected with, 106
discipline, 97
dolls, children's reaction to, 98
dynamics, 76, 77

E

earth, teaching about as a living organism, 67–69
education
    appealing to whole child, 97
    coming from mental attitude, 42
    comprehending with whole human being, 4
    contradictions in discussing, 43–44
    early, 37
    golden rules of, 56–57
    guiding children in soul and spirit, 47
    inner life as ground of, 13
    judging, 84
    spirit as basis of, 4
    spiritual science giving life to, 135
    teaching at service of, 58
    too much discussion about, 131–32, 133
Education of the Child in the Light of Anthroposophy, The (Steiner), 36
elementary school, avoiding sudden transition to, 58
environment, struggle with heredity, 46–47
esthetic judgement, nurturing, 52–53
ether body, 80
eurythmy, 87, 97
    artistic representations of, 115–16
    as art of movement, 116–17, 118
    expressions of, 118–19
    facial expressions with, 118
    feeling in, 117, 118
    figures for, 120
    unconscious momentum in, 117
    veil of, 117, 119
    as visible speech, 116, 119–20
    volition in, 117, 118
    wood figures, 116–17
evolution, 36, 132
experimentation, 20
external world, proper time to teach about, 66
eye
    physiological operation of, 7
    transparency of, 29

F

fainting of soul, 23
fanaticism, 133–34
fatigue, resulting from limited appeal to rhythmic system, 51
feeling
    in eurythmy, 117, 118
    related to breathing and blood circulation, 38–39, 45
    related to rhythmic system, 38–39
feelings
    perceived as ideas, 39
    universe connected with human beings through, 69
finite concepts, effect on brain, 128–29
form, 102, 103
freedom, respect for, 57

G

geography, 102, 104
girls, 108, 122, 124
God
    acting on intentions of, 5
    breathing of, 22
gout, from overloaded memory, 69–70
grammar, 96
gratitude, 54, 57, 113
greensickness, 109 n.1
growth, 66, 121
gymnastics exercises, 86–87

H

Haeckel, Ernst, 14
handwork, 97–101
hard thinking, effect on brain, 128
harmony, educating towards, 47
head, inactive in phlegmatic children, 80
healing, pedagogical, 80
heredity, struggle with environment, 46–47
higher knowledge, beginning with childhood body, 33
historical images, 76, 77
How to Know Higher Worlds (Steiner), 24, 32
human anatomy class, 98
human being
    each a fresh problem, 130
    earlier ages with greater understanding of, 132
    knowledge of, 2–3
    knowledge and science focused on, 133
    loss of being, 132
    spirit of, 3
    threefold nature of, 44–45
    viewed unfavorably, 133
human growth, suddenness of, 125
human nature, basing true teaching and pedagogy on, 35
human science, 37
human systems, development of, 45
humor, 78, 82
Huxley, Thomas H., 3

I

ideas
    connected to antipathy, 128
    sifting through the head, 85–87
    stuck in the head, 84–85, 86–87
ideation, connected with nervous system, 38
illness
    approach to, 11
    love of, 94
imagery
    children learning through, 14, 34
    children taking as much as is bearable, 70
imagination, 24
imagination, children learning through, 14
immortality, 25–26, 34
individuality, 78–79, 84–85
inner world, enigmatic to boys, 124
inspiration, ruling children, 13
instruction time, economy of, 64–65

intellect, 20, 21
    calling too early, 13
    image of spirit, 18
    unreality of, 23
    working of, 25–26
intellectualism, 127
intellectual knowledge, 8
intellectual precepts, awakening to, 52–53
interest, failure to arouse, 109
intuitional cognition, 8–9

J

judgment, 24–25

K

kidneys, affected by grief, 49
knowledge, 24

L

language, 96
    importance to teenage boys, 122–23, 124
    spirit and soul hidden in, 16–17
larynx, 116
learning, slow, 61
letters, unconnected to young children's nature, 58–59
life
    considering when teaching, 33–35
    surrendering to flow of, 31
limb system, related to volition, 40, 45
liver, importance of, 107–8
logic, 13, 24, 77

M

materialism, 123, 129
materialistic science, failures in perception, 49
mathematics, 70–73
mechanics, 75, 76, 77
melancholic children, 79–80, 83, 107
memory, effects of overloading, 69–70
metabolism, related to movement and volition, 40–41
mind, distinct from spirit, 17–18
mineralogy, 75
modeling, related to rhythmic system, 50
Molt, Emil, 2, 35, 89–90
moral education, 129
moral principles, link to arithmetic, 70–73
morals, 53
moral teaching, 51–52, 97, 113
movement
    change in source of as children grow, 75
    related to metabolism and volition, 40–41
muscular system, 74, 76
music, 50, 97
musical education, foundation for will, 62
mystery of the universe, solution to, 130

N

natural science, 2–3, 36–37
nature, studying without regard to spiritual, 3
needlework, 101

nervous system
    affected in pubescent boys, 122, 124
    ideation connected with, 38
    related to thinking, 40, 45
neuritis, 109

O

observation, 24–25
opinions, 134
organism
    school as, 88–89, 95
    working in harmony with, 79–83
organs, built according to physical manifestations taken in, 46
outer environment, living in, 23–24
outer world, enigmatic to girls, 124
Outline of Esoteric Science, An (Steiner), 32

P

painting, 50, 101
paleness, in children, 39, 42
passivity, 18, 22
Paul, Jean, 33
philosophy, ending in gratitude, 54
phlegmatic temperament, 80–81, 83
physical, promoting through spiritual work, 47
physical education, continuous nature of, 37
physical life, connecting spirituality with, 109–10

physics, 75, 76
pictorial element, teaching through, 60, 65
plant kingdom, 76, 77
play, 106
points of view, 134
practical life, 97–98, 101
proletarian children, 90
psychology, 3
    educational testing, 51
    without soul, 38
puberty
    acquiring own mind and spirit after, 37
    facing difficulties directly, 121

R

reading, following writing, 59, 62
recitation, 86
religious denominations, 3
religious instruction, 96–97, 113–15
representational painting, 102
reverence, teachers' need for, 54, 57
rheumatism, from overloaded memory, 69–70
rhythmic system
    affected by art, 50–51
    dominant in sanguine children, 81
    fatigue resulting from limited appeal to, 51
    predominant between seventh year and puberty, 50
    related to disposition, 74
    related to feeling, 38–39, 45

Riddles of the Soul (Steiner), 35–36
right arm/hand,
    movements of, 7–8

S

sadness, related to mouth dryness, 45
salt, overabundance causing melancholy, 79
sanguine temperament, 81, 83, 107–8
school
    continuous study of, 92–93
    need to understand students, 89–90
    need to understand teachers, 89
school doctor, 105
Schubert, Karl, 112
scientific spiritual observation, on child's taste, 41–42
self-awareness, physiological foundation for, 128
self-denial. *See* asceticism
senses, dominant in phlegmatic children, 81
sexes, differences between, 100, 121–22, 124
singing, 86, 97, 129
skeletal system, 74–75, 76–77
skeleton, soul and spirit reaching into, 75
sleep, 5, 7
sleeping/waking cycle, part of rhythmic system, 39
society, preparing children to stay in touch with, 91
solitude, 30
song, arrested movements in, 116

soul
    becoming through breathing, 22
    changes in during life, 31
    in child's nature, 16
    fainting in, 23
    feeling manifesting physically as rhythms of breathing and circulation, 41
    leaving impression on body, 19
    leaving physical body, 34
    perceived in expressions, 18, 19
    play as free expression of, 106
    removing hindrances from, 56
    seeking reality of, 18
    thought manifesting physically as nervous activity, 41
    vowels expressing, 16–17
soul experience, from color experience, 104
soul life, basis for education, 38
soul understanding, goal of, 76
sounds, learned through eurythmy, 119–20
space, 103
speech organs, extending movement through whole human being, 116
speech, 6, 7–8, 116, 120
spinning, 101
spirit
    absorbing lessons concerning, 37
    acting with, 14
    action of in human being, 132

active, 22
attaining, 20
basis of education, 4
becoming visible, 32
call to work with, 4
in child's nature, 16
close to body in children, 4
consonants expressing, 16–17
as creator, 49–50
distinct from mind, 17–18
entering, 27
knowledge of in community's practical life, 4
lacking knowledge how to use, 4
meaning of, 15–16
perceived in reflections, 18, 19
perceiving when physical activity is suppressed, 28–29
removing hindrances from, 56
weaving continuously in physical, 53
working of, 25–27
spiritual approach, need for, 23
spiritual culture, shortcomings of, 3
spiritual forces, molding human body, 4
spirituality, connecting with physical life, 109–10
spiritual life, 2, 28
spiritual observation, 40
spiritual-physiological pedagogy, 12
spiritual science, 114–15, 123, 129, 131
contribution of, 49
goal of, 134–35
spiritual truths, 35–36
spiritual views, confirmation of, 123
Steiner, Rudolf, family teacher, 64–65
students, meeting with on equal terms, 127
sugar, related to disposition, 107
suprasensory world, 3, 122

T

taste, child-adult differences in, 41–42
teachers
ability to assess child's health, 105
adopting spiritual standpoint, 129–30
approach to educating more intelligent children, 48
artistic approach of, 94
convenience of triviality to, 33
cooperating in spiritual creation, 106
deep relationship with children, 112–13
flexibility of ideas and feelings, 77
friendliness and love for children, 78
gratitude as primary mood for teaching young children, 55, 57
having artists' understanding of children, 77, 83, 84
humor needed, 78, 82, 84

importance of understanding whole human being, 74
individual children, love of, 94–95
mediators between divine order and children, 10
need for open worldview, 127
observing spirit at work in bodily nature, 4–5
preparation of, 63, 65
primary task, 48–49
recognizing individuality, 78–79, 84–85
relationships with teenage students, 125–26
secret of training, 125
self-perception needed, 48
staff meetings, 93–94, 95
training in receptivity to changes in human nature, 124–25
treating children in spiritual way, 33
understanding as individuals, 89
understanding temperaments, 79
working from philosophy of life, 131

teaching
considering whole of life, 33–35
goal of, 105
humor and congeniality preferred over logic, 10
individuality of, 61, 84–85
love for, 55
means of educating, 58
need to be aware of each age's requirements, 10–11

teeth, change of, 9, 47
temperaments, 78–84
thinking, related to nervous system, 40, 45
thought forces, strengthening, 32
toys, children's creations, 97–99

U

unhappiness, countering, 53
unity, 71–72
universal view, 53–54
upper classes, difficulties with physical health, 108–9

V

variety, 61–62
vocal transformation, 123
volition
    assaulting nervous system, 124
    in eurythmy, 117, 118
    related to metabolism and movement, 40–41
vowels, 16–17, 119

W

Waldorf school
    aim of, 110, 111
    basis for training of staff, 37–38
    Christian character of, 115
    color source of special attention in, 85–86
    dealing with educational authorities, 91–92
    establishment of, 2
    founding of, 89–90
    goal of, 42, 91
    goal of teaching, 105

growth of, 95
individuality of teaching in,
    61, 84–85
organization of, 88, 91
policy of not keeping
    children back, 112
principles of, 2
progress reports on children,
    110–11
schedule, 95–96
single teacher responsible for
    group of students, 87
special class, 112–13
special pedagogy not
    cultivated, 133
teachers necessary for, 36
teachers' need to love
    teaching, 56
teacher staff meetings, 93–94
training teachers in
    receptivity to changes in
    human nature, 124–25
valuing pedagogy and
    teaching over
    structure, 111
weaving, 101
will, strengthening, 32
wisdom, love of, 133
woodwork classes, 97
writing, 58–61

Y

yoga, 20–23
young children
    art of educating, 43–57
    need for teachers with
        gratitude, 55, 57

DURING THE LAST TWO DECADES of the nineteenth century the Austrian-born Rudolf Steiner (1861–1925) became a respected and well-published scientific, literary, and philosophical scholar, particularly known for his work on Goethe's scientific writings. After the turn of the century, he began to develop his earlier philosophical principles into a methodical approach to the research of psychological and spiritual phenomena.

His multifaceted genius led to innovative and holistic approaches in medicine, science, education (Waldorf schools), special education, philosophy, religion, agriculture (biodynamic farming), architecture, drama, movement (eurythmy), speech, and other fields. In 1924 he founded the General Anthroposophical Society, which has branches throughout the world.